Great Gardens of
SPAIN

Great Gardens of
SPAIN

Anneli Bojstad
PHOTOGRAPHY by Eduardo Mencos

F
FRANCES LINCOLN LIMITED
PUBLISHERS

Frances Lincoln Limited
4 Torriano Mews
Torriano Avenue
London NW5 2RZ
www.franceslincoln.com

Great Gardens of Spain
Copyright © Frances Lincoln Limited 2011
Text copyright © Anneli Bojstad 2011
Photographs © Eduardo Mencos 2011
First Frances Lincoln edition 2011

A catalogue record for this book is available from the
British Library.

ISBN 978-0-7112-2671-5

Printed and bound in China

1 2 3 4 5 6 7 8 9

CONTENTS

Atlantic

Pazo de Mariñán, La Coruña
Monasterio de San Lorenzo de Trasouto,
  Santiago de Compostela
Pazo de Castrelos, Vigo
La Quinta, Cudillero
Señorío de Bértiz, Oieregi Bertizarana
Jardín de Aclimatación de la Orotava, Tenerife
Jardín de la Marquesa de Arucas, Gran Canaria
Jardín de Cactus, Lanzarote

The Centre

Palacio Real de la Granja de San Ildelfonso, Segovia
El Romeral de San Marcos, Segovia
El Bosque, Béjar
Real Monasterio de San Lorenzo de El Escorial
Casita del Infante, San Lorenzo de El Escorial
Casita del Príncipe, San Lorenzo de El Escorial
La Quinta del Duque del Arco, Madrid
Jardines del Buen Retiro, Madrid
Jardín de Joaquín Sorolla, Madrid
Real Jardín Botánico, Madrid
El Capricho, Madrid
Real Sitio de Aranjuez, Aranjuez
Jardín de la Real Fábrica de Paños, Brihuega
Monasterio de Piedra, Nuévalos

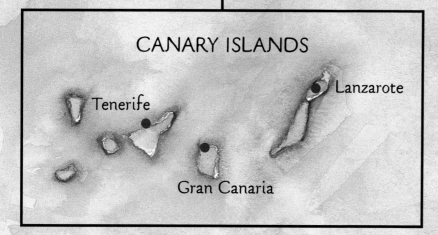

CANARY ISLANDS

Tenerife

Lanzarote

Gran Canaria

Andalusia

El Patio de los Naranjos, Córdoba
Palacio de Viana, Córdoba
La Alhambra, Granada
El Generalife, Granada
Carmen de la Fundación Rodríguez Acosta,
  Granada
Real Alcázar, Seville
La Casa de Pilatos, Seville
El Parque de María Luisa, Seville
La Casa del Rey Moro, Ronda
La Concepción, Málaga

BAY OF BISCAY

La Coruña
Cudillero
Santiago de Compostela
Vigo
Oieregi Bertizarana

La Pobla de Lillet

Nuévalos

Barcelona

Segovia
Brihuega

Cambrils

El Escorial

Béjar

MADRID

Menorca

Aranjuez

Mallorca

Valencia

Elche

MEDITERRANEAN SEA

Córdoba

Sevilla

Granada

Málaga

Ronda

STRAIT OF GIBRALTAR

Mediterranean

Jardines Artigas, La Pobla de Lillet
Park Güell, Barcelona
Laberinto de Horta, Barcelona
Parque Samá, Cambrils
Jardín de Montforte, Valencia
Huerto del Cura, Elche
Raixa, Mallorca
Alfabia, Mallorca
Pedreres de S'Hostal, Menorca

INTRODUCTION

When I visited Spain for the first time almost a quarter of a century ago, the gardens fascinated me, particularly the Andalusian patios with their riot of colours and scents, so far removed from anything I had known in my native Sweden. Like many northern pilgrims to the fabled south, I was seduced by these marvellous spaces, created to exalt the senses, embodying the concept of a garden as a re-creation of paradise, closed off from the outside world.

Originating in the Middle East, the paradise garden is well suited to the climate and landscape of a large part of the Iberian Peninsula, but it is completely alien to the misty green lands of northern Spain, where gardens follow an English model, opening themselves to their surroundings. Paradise there is more like an Arcadian pastoral. Diversity of climate and landscape is surely the essence of Spain and its gardens, together with a complex history – a crucible of different cultures and civilizations. The gardens – products of their times – bear witness to this extraordinary adventure.

The story of Spain's gardens begins in the Roman period, lasting from the second century BC to the sixth century AD, when Hispania was a prosperous imperial province. From the atrium and peristyle comes the patio, considered to be the soul of the Spanish garden. The spectacular fountains in the excavated gardens of Itálica and Mérida show the Roman mastery of the art of hydraulics, and are precursors to the dramatic water features of the Renaissance and Baroque. Another important legacy from this period is topiary, the art of training trees and shrubs into any form.

While the gardens of Hispania were much like those in other corners of the empire, products of the globalization inherent in Roman culture, the gardens created when the Moors held sway are unique, fruits of the encounter between the Romanized West and the Arab invaders from the East. Spain's Islamic era began in the year 711 and lasted for more than eight centuries, leaving a legacy of universally famous Hispano-Islamic gardens, including the Patio de los Naranjos in Córdoba and the Alhambra in Granada. The Moors developed the Romans' sophisticated water engineering techniques and introduced new plants, including orange and lemon trees. Another enduring characteristic is the mixture of ornamental and productive species. The quartered gardens with low pools, irrigation channels and tiled walkways are the very image of Spanish gardens today.

Detail of the Jardín de Joaquín Sorolla. Jets of water, tiles and pots of flowers are the essential elements of a traditional Spanish garden.

During this time of Moorish domination, another quite different reality co-existed on the Iberian Peninsula: Christian Spain, with its cruciform monastic gardens. The paths crossing the Islamic garden were a metaphor for the Koran's four rivers of paradise, while for Christians they were a representation of the four rivers of the biblical paradise, of the four evangelists, the four cardinal virtues. Here, once again, is the recurring idea that the garden is a space that symbolizes paradise, for both Christianity and Islam. The fusion of garden and paradise already existed in the Greco-Roman tradition, in the evocation of the Elysian Fields where heroes passed a happy afterlife among meadows of flowers.

In 1492 the last Muslim kingdom in Iberia, Granada, fell to the Catholic monarchs Ferdinand and Isabella. Spain was unified and the Renaissance began, fuelled by new influences from the Spanish dominions of Sicily, Naples and Milan. Classical elements including flights of stairs, loggias and grottoes were added to the indigenous tradition, giving birth to such emblematic spaces as the gardens of the Real Alcázar in Seville (see page 218). The influence of Flanders, another of the Crown's dominions, is evident in Philip II's garden at Aranjuez (see page 166) with its small flower beds, bowers wreathed with vines and green galleries, converted in the seventeenth and eighteenth centuries into a great Italianate salon for grand celebrations and baroque spectacle. Here is the garden as a place for pleasure, for dreams and their fulfilment.

Another deep mark was left by the discovery of America and the consequent introduction of new ornamental species which transformed the gardens of the Spanish court. These included tuberose (*Polianthes tuberosa*), the four o'clock flower

Pergolas such as those at La Concepción (left) and La Casa de Pilatos (right) are marvellous green refuges full of scents, shade and fresh air.

(*Mirabilis jalaba*), garden nasturtium (*Tropaeolum majus*) and the tomato which, like the sunflower, was originally grown for its aesthetic value and was not appreciated as a foodstuff until much later, being originally regarded as poisonous. Centuries later, Enlightenment Spain led the world in botany. Under the reign of the Bourbons, expeditions were dispatched to the New World and botanical gardens were founded to acclimatize the exotic treasures.

This new French dynasty installed at the start of the eighteenth century brought with it a French garden style whose symmetry and long perspectives expressed the absolute power of the monarch. As can be seen in the gardens at La Granja (see page 104), this new style did not entirely replace the indigenous tradition, which tended to fragment large spaces into intimate corners, a legacy of the Moors and Romans. The landscape garden was introduced to Spain towards the end of this century; but despite interesting examples such as El Capricho (page 160), this style did not take root, as the parched Spanish landscape was largely unsuited to the pastoral scenes evoked by the great parks that surrounded English country houses; and in any case the Spanish nobility did not tend to live in their country estates.

The nineteenth century began with the disastrous Peninsular War against the French, which was also the ruin of many historical gardens. New gardens created later in the century followed the eclecticism fashionable throughout Europe, and it was not until the appearance of the marvellous Antonio Gaudí that Spain once again made a wholly unique contribution to the world of garden design. Created at the start of the twentieth century, Park Güell (see page 58) was the fruit of Gaudí's spiritual journey and his longing to make a new Eden, where

man could once again meet God. The connection between garden and paradise flows like an underground river through the history of gardens from their earliest beginnings.

This book is a partial tour of the gardens of Spain, which are one of the world's great treasures. Many of the gardens here are nothing less than an earthly paradise, and all are open to the curious visitor. That has been the basis of my selection, in itself an essentially subjective task: these places each have their own special character, and they can all be visited. The book sprang from a desire to share my great pleasure in visiting these places, with a brief text to make it easier to interpret the gardens, placing them in a historical, cultural and social context.

In the same way that gardens are influenced by other gardens, books owe much to other books. I am indebted to the Marquesa de Casa Valdés' magnificent *Gardens of Spain*, which has been a constant point of reference during my travels. Thanks to Eduardo Mencos' extraordinary photos, which convey the spirit of the gardens at different stages of the year, you can take this tour of Spanish gardens without leaving your armchair. But I urge you not to stay there, and I hope that the book whets your appetite for a visit. Gardens are living entities, constantly evolving.

Madrid, December 2010

Classical influences are at the heart of the eighteenth-century garden of Laberinto de Horta.

The Atlantic

PAZO DE MARIÑÁN
La Coruña, Galicia

As soon as you step out on to the magnificent terrace of the Pazo de Mariñán, the spectacle begins: an exhilarating dialogue between the formal geometry of the parterre and the natural setting of the Betanzos estuary. The garden's design perfectly incorporates the estuary, appropriating its surroundings as an extraordinary focal point – what the Japanese describe as *shakkei* or 'borrowed landscape'.

A few miles from La Coruña, the *pazo* was built as a stronghold by the nobleman Gómez Pérez das Mariñas in the fifteenth century. But its current appearance as a palatial mansion owes more to the second half of the eighteenth century, when such typically baroque touches as balustrades, stairs and granite statues were added. In fact, the Galician word *pazo* derives from the Latin *palatium*, meaning 'a noble country house'. Set among fields and forests, and enveloped in a haze of nostalgia, *pazos* have come to form part of Galicia's natural and cultural landscape.

What was originally a productive garden was transformed in the early nineteenth century into an ornamental garden, with the great parterre at its heart. Designed to be seen from

A filigree of box hedges spreading from the house's rear façade makes an orderly green carpet.

above, box hedges form a carpet of elaborate arabesques, following the French *broderie* model. Inspired by the lacework of the period, this style was enormously popular through the Renaissance and Baroque periods. It is thought that the garden's designer was the Frenchman Mathias Thiebe, who came to Galicia with Napoleon's invading armies.

Extending to either side of a central axis there is a landscape garden, the product of the romantic spirit of the nineteenth century, when many exotic species were introduced. These include the monumental *Eucalyptus globulus* at the entrance, said to be the first grown in Spain, with seeds sent by the Galician bishop Rosendo Salvador from the mission he founded at New Norcia in Australia.

The *pazo* passed through the generations from father to son until 1936, when the last owner, Gerardo Bermúdez de Castro, died childless, and ownership passed to the local government of La Coruña.

Fusing the aesthetic and the practical, the rural and the sophisticated, the agricultural and the ornamental, this emblematic place seems to have grown over the centuries to represent many of the region's own idiosyncrasies.

Above Decorative and architectural elements in granite are an essential feature of Galicia's gardens.

Right A detail of the large parterre, where low box hedges form the shapes of flowers, stars and shields.

MONASTERIO DE SAN LORENZO DE TRASOUTO
Santiago de Compostela, Galicia

San Lorenzo's greatest treasure is undoubtedly this cloister with its imposing green architecture of formal box hedges, which according to the owners are some four hundred years old. These are exceptional examples of the ancient *ars topiaria*, the art of training trees and bushes. The Roman writer Pliny the Elder used this term in his *Natural History* to refer to the art of gardening in general, which, following Greek antecedents, he regarded as the imposition of form on nature. Pliny describes how the shears of the *topiarus*, or gardener, sculpt the evergreen box, yew and cypress into figures, architectural forms and even letters – as still occurs at San Lorenzo twice every year.

Here one finds Christian symbols such as the alpha and the omega, the acronym IHS – Iesus Hominum Salvator or Jesus, Saviour of Mankind – and the Cross of Calatrava, the pre-eminent symbol of Iberian knighthood. Apart from the space occupied by a fountain and a statue of the Virgin, the patio is dominated by these powerful hedges, which are grouped in squares.

This is a spiritual garden: closed off from the hubbub of everyday life, and open only to the sky, it is designed to turn one's attention inward, to the garden of the soul.

With its huge sculpted hedges, this cloistered garden in the pilgrim city of Santiago de Compostela exemplifies nature being controlled by man. It is also a restful place, removed from the haphazard natural world and imbued with symbols of the Catholic faith.

One of the shapes formed by the green sea of hedges is a grill, the symbol of San Lorenzo, who was martyred on a bonfire. The hermitage originally here was dedicated to this saint in the thirteenth century, and later became a Franciscan monastery. In the fifteenth century this came into the ownership of the Counts of Altamira, who kept some rooms for spiritual retreat; their guests included the Emperor Charles V, who spent Holy Week here in 1520. Converted into a palace in the nineteenth century, the property remains in the Altamira family.

Above A fifteenth-century statue of the Virgin crowns the spring in this monastic garden.

Right and opposite A view from the upper gallery shows the high, dense box hedges, which form religious symbols including the Cross of Calatrava, the Cross of Jerusalem and St James's scallop shell.

PAZO DE CASTRELOS

Vigo, Galicia

'The palace and garden had the ancient, melancholy grandeur of places where days were whiled away in the pursuits of courtly love.' The phrase *Sonata de Otoño* (autumn sonata), the title of a novel by the Galician author Ramón María del Valle-Inclán, encapsulates the romantic spirit of the Pazo de Castrelos, a country manor which has been absorbed by the city of Vigo.

As with many of Galicia's *pazos*, the story of Castrelos begins with a medieval fortified tower – Lavandeira. This was destroyed in a war with neighbouring Portugal in the seventeenth century. The new building begun in 1670 acquired its current shape in the late nineteenth and early twentieth centuries, when the battlements, towers and lookout posts which give it the air of an ancient fortress were added, in the historicist fashion of that era.

Dating from the same period, the garden is strikingly eclectic, a synthesis of several different styles.

There are three distinct spaces on different levels: a formal garden in front of the house, with geometric box hedges; a rose garden laid out in straight lines on the upper level; and on the lower level a landscape park, known as the La Pradera de Té, the Tea Lawn, with winding paths and a pond.

This compartmentalized layout is typical of *pazos* from this period in Galicia, where the rolling terrain lends itself to terraced designs. It is believed that this garden was designed by Jacintho Mattos from the nearby Portuguese city of Oporto. Many of the exotic trees typical of the era were planted here at the end of the nineteenth century, *Magnolia grandiflora*, *Liriodendron tulipifera*, *Araucaria angustifolia* and *Eucalyptus globulus* among them. Thanks to the climate of Spain's north-west coast, mild and wet all year long, these have grown to an enormous size.

The emblematic species of the Galician garden is undoubtedly the magical camellia. With its spectacular flowers, it is the star of any garden in the winter months and, although it originated in Japan and China, it is now so intimately linked with the Galician landscape that hardly anyone would consider it exotic.

The Pazo de Castrelos is also known as Quiñones de León, after its last owner, who left it to the city of Vigo. It was opened as a museum in 1937. Though boxed in by the traffic and tarmac of the modern city, this green jewel is still redolent of past glories.

Left Box hedges form the basis of the French-inspired garden to the rear of the house.

Above A magnificent specimen of *Camellia japonica* thrives beyond the triangles, ovals and trapezoids of the hedges.

Right In the landscape garden a model of the *pazo* occupies an island in the pond. *Far right* Detail of a fountain in granite, the archetypal stone of Galicia.

LA QUINTA
Cudillero, Asturias

'We must cultivate our own garden,' Voltaire concluded in *Candide*. However bad the world may be, with hard work we can improve our immediate surroundings and create our own private paradise. This is exactly what the Selgas brothers achieved with the extraordinary combination of architecture and landscape they created, between1880 and 1895, at La Quinta in their native Asturias, far from Spain's cultural capitals. They set out not only to delight and satisfy their own spirits but also to enrich society. Their motto was: 'To provide culture is to serve the nation.'

Brothers Ezequiel and Fortunato Selgas (1828–1909 and 1839–1921) were born into a well-to-do merchant family in the coastal village of Cudillero. Ezequiel, the elder, moved to Madrid and thanks to a good nose for business was able to amass a large fortune in a short time. His younger brother, Fortunato, was thus able to receive a superb liberal education, and dedicated himself to fine art. The house at La Quinta was built to his design, though for legal reasons it was necessary to credit a friendly qualified architect for the work. Fortunato also made the initial designs for the garden, in keeping with the eclectic style of the buildings. Because of their frequent travel abroad, particularly to Paris, the

Selgas brothers were aware of the latest developments in both architecture and landscape design.

Ezequiel had begun in 1860 to acquire the works of art which today form the magnificent collection on display at La Quinta, which was the family's summer residence until the death of the last surviving descendant in 1992. Since then, the house and garden have been cared for by the Selgas-Fagalde Foundation, which has preserved it exactly as it was. The admirable conservation effort extends to the gardens, which offer a faithful representation of the original design, as the foundation has not introduced any new elements and has restricted itself to maintenance and, where necessary, replacement with identical plants. It could be said that the garden at La Quinta is a real museum piece, a living treasure from the past where time stands still.

Two French garden designers worked alongside Fortunato: Grandpont and, later, Jean Pierre Rigoreau. Typically for its period, the garden at La Quinta is made up of several gardens, each with its own character, following French, Italian and English models, and expressing the brothers' enjoyment of what they had seen on their travels. Your first impression is formed, even before

With hedges of *Camellia japonica* to either side, a Versailles-style avenue runs from the main house, contrasting with the surrounding rural landscape.

entering the garden, by the avenue that extends from the south façade of the palace like a great green carpet, embroidered in summer with flowers. The horizontal plane of this *tapis vert* contrasts with vertical walls of *Camellia japonica*, which reinforce the sense of perspective and create a monumental frame for the façade, the vanishing point of the composition. Following the French baroque model, the space is filled with sculpture, urns and fountains.

While the French garden is open and dynamic, the Italian garden to the rear of the palace is secluded and intimate, defined by the buildings that surround it on all four sides. This garden, with a low pool at the centre, is determined and given order by architectural elements which include steps, walls, balustrades and terraces.

The English garden lies to the east of the house. Here the geometrical rigour of the other areas gives way to irregular lines and wide lawns, with groups of exotic trees (*Sequoia sempervivens, Acer palmatum, Thujopsis dolabrata, Liriodendron tulipifera, Phyllostachys nigra*). Water defines this ideal landscape, forming a series of ponds in an encircling river. Completing the romantic scene is an artificial grotto crowned by a classical temple.

Above all, you feel here the majesty of the trees, opulent creatures of the mild, damp climate in this rainy corner of northern Spain.

Above left and right The Italian garden, which is focused on a low pool, has a pavilion on either side and an abundance of architectural features.

Left and below right The landscape garden is shaped by undulating streams and vast trees including sequoias, tulip trees (*Liriodendron tulipifera*) and maples.

Above right At the far end of the large pond is a grotto crowned with a temple.

SEÑORÍO DE BÉRTIZ
Oieregi-Bertizarana, Navarra

'Consult the genius of the place in all; that tells the waters or to rise, or fall,' wrote the English poet Alexander Pope in 1731, arguing that a garden should fit the spirit of its place, its *genius loci*, its essence, which affects all the senses. True to this principle – one of the pillars of the landscape designer's art – the romantic garden of the Señorío de Bértiz is profoundly connected to its location: an unforgettable part of north-east Navarra, where the Pyrenees descend to the sea, surrounded by immense forests of beech, oak and alder, and enveloped in the mists of a mild damp climate.

The history of the feudal estate of Señorío de Bértiz begins in the fourteenth century with the first owner, Pedro Miguel de Bértiz. He was granted hereditary dominion over some 2,000 hectares, the inhabitants, and their income and property, and until 1811 his descendants also held jurisdiction there. The *señorío* passed through the generations until 1884. Although it appears that parts of the garden are from the mid-nineteenth century, its current form dates from the time of the last owner, Pedro Ciga, who bought it in 1898 and left it in 1948 to the Diputación Foral de Navarra.

Above Honeysuckle and wisteria cover this arbour, which is constructed in concrete to imitate branches.

Right Black bamboo stands out among the exotic vegetation around the pond.

Entering the garden you step into a dreamlike and nostalgic atmosphere. Winding paths are mute guides leading to the picturesque scenes of an artificial lake with islets, bridges, a waterfall and a concrete pavilion. Glades of different varieties of bamboo (*Phyllostachys nigra* and *P. viridiglaucescens*) lend a Japanese air. The microclimate here allows garden trees to flourish, creating a green cathedral full of ginkgo, sequoia, taxodium, yew, sweet gum, cedar, araucaria and cryptomeria.

While the main house is a good example of traditional regional architecture, the eye is drawn to an Art Nouveau chapel, with its pergola and a magnificent belvedere in the same style, by the river Bidasoa. With its constant murmur, the river is an essential element in this garden, bringing to mind Borges' beautiful lines:

To gaze at the river made of time and water
And recall that time itself is another river,
To know we cease to be, just like the river,
And that our faces pass away, just like the water.

Above and right The chapel and the riverside belvedere are two Art Nouveau gems.

Above Dating from 1847, the main house is built in the traditional style of the region.

Left and above The romantic landscape garden surrounding the artificial lake is transformed by the changing seasons; the fresh green tones of spring give way to autumn's warmer tints.

JARDÍN DE ACLIMATACIÓN DE LA OROTAVA

Puerto de La Cruz, Tenerife

'The Spanish government, possessed of the most beautiful corners of the earth, is the only one which could bring together in a favourable climate the most precious tropical plants and acclimatize them for temperate zones.' So wrote the French botanist André Pierre Ledru, who prepared the first catalogue of plants grown in this garden, which was founded by royal decree in 1788 for the new and useful species that Spanish sailors and scientists were discovering in the New World.

The garden was the creation of Alonso de Nava y Grimón, the 6th Marquis of Villanueva de Prado, who took on almost every responsibility, from choosing the site to financing it, without other recompense than the honour of serving his king and country. As befits the empirical spirit of the age, the marquis carried out tests with exotic seeds in different locations before settling on the Orotava valley to the north of Tenerife as the site. Work began in 1791, following plans by the Canarian architect Diego Nicolás Eduardo; later Ledru and his compatriot the draftsman Le Gros organized the gardens along Linnean principles.

The two Frenchmen formed part of a 1796 expedition to Trinidad, which was almost lost at sea in a terrible storm. With their ship foundering, they miraculously survived and, making for land, arrived at Tenerife, where they spent four months exploring the island while their ship was repaired. As he relates in his *Voyage to Tenerife*, Ledru was captivated by the island. 'If I had to abandon the land of my birth and chose another home, it would be in the Fortunate Isles, it would be in La Orotava, that I would choose to lead the rest of my life.'

On completion, the garden immediately began to receive plants from expeditions organized by the Spanish Crown in order to classify the botanical riches of its empire and collect species of medicinal, agricultural and industrial interest. The naturalists and artists who undertook these adventures underwent many hardships, and often risked their lives for science. Towards the end of the eighteenth century there were three exclusively Spanish botanical expeditions to America: to Peru, to Nueva Granada (modern-day Colombia) and to Nueva España (Mexico and Central America). One of the era's most sought-after plants, still to be found in the garden today, was the quinine tree (*Cinchona officinalis*), from which the crucial remedy for malaria and other ailments could be extracted. Another medicinal plant, originating in Colombia and studied by the great botanist Celestino Mutis, was coca (*Erythroxylon coca*), brought into the garden alongside comestibles such as the Andean cherimoya or custard apple (*Annona cherimolia*) and the Mexican papaya (*Carica papaya*).

Right A spider plant (*Chlorophytum comosum 'Variegatum'*) and *Clivia miniata* set off a screwpine (*Pandanus utilis*).

Opposite The enormous banyan tree (*Ficus macrophylla* ssp. *columnaris*) is like a prehistoric beast.

Following pages Waterlilies glow in the pool.

The staggering range of new species discovered by the Spanish botanists went on to transform the gardens of all Europe in the century that followed. Among these were araucarias, jacarandas, daturas, spikenards and dahlias, all of which and many others passed through La Orotava and then on to other royal gardens.

Similar acclimatization gardens were created in the peninsula's greatest ports, including Cádiz, Puerto de Santamaría, Valencia and Cartagena. Orotava remained the most successful of them all, because of the compatibility of the climate of the Canaries with that of the American tropics, although usually plants did not survive the harsh dry winters of Castile when they were transferred to the royal palaces at Aranjuez, La Granja or Madrid.

Today Orotava is a sanctuary for more than two thousand species of tropical and subtropical plants from five continents. They are presided over by a spectacular *Ficus macrophylla*. Originally from Australia, this giant with its impressive aerial roots makes a fantasmagorical sight. There is no other place in Europe where the magical ambience of the tropics is so present, where trade winds breathe warm and damp on your skin, carrying you to exotic climes without lifting you from the old continent.

The pond with arches of bamboo.

JARDÍN DE LA MARQUESA DE ARUCAS
Arucas, Gran Canaria

It is not hard to believe that the ancient Greeks placed the mythical Garden of the Hesperides in the Canary Islands. Here in Arucas, where the plants flourish and the climate is like eternal spring, you feel transported to that earthly paradise, where the trees put forth golden apples of immortality, cared for by the nymphs called the Hesperides, who were guarded by the fierce hundred-headed dragon Ladon. According to myth, even though the dragon was slain by the titan Atlas, its descendants are still alive in the shape of the dragon trees (*Dracaena draco*) that sprang up where its blood fell. One magnificent 200-year-old specimen dominates the old part of this garden. When the bark is broken, a dark red sap leaks out – 'dragon's blood', possessed of curative properties. Sacred to the indigenous Canarians, the Guanches, the tree is still symbolic of the Canary Islands.

Covering 5 hectares near Las Palmas, the garden is divided into old and new parts. The old part was designed by a French landscape architect around 1880 to complement the house built for the 1st Marquis of Arucas, Ramón Madam y Uriondo. Thanks to the tropical climate, this outdoor room was used all the year round. The layout follows nineteenth-century convention with paths – covered with the local lava – that wind through irregularly shaped borders.

Left A picturesque nineteenth-century pavilion.

Right This pond with its jungle-like atmosphere is close to the house.

Left An impressive example of the legendary dragon tree (*Dracaena draco*), which has become the symbol of the Canary Islands.

Below A space characterized by ferns and tree ferns.

Picturesque touches include a moss-clad grotto and a lakeside pavilion. A folly in the shape of a castle, doubling as a viewpoint, crowns an artificial mountain.

The marquis, founder of a prosperous local sugar refinery, was an enthusiastic botanist, and the collection of araucarias surrounding the house is part of his legacy.

Sheltered by the side of a mountain, the Montaña de Arucas, and with the sea close at hand, the garden enjoys a generous microclimate that has allowed these and other exotic trees including jacarandas, rubber plants and chorisias to flourish.

In 1990 the family extended the garden and opened it to the public. To complete the display of tropical and subtropical species begun by the 1st Marquis, hundreds of varieties of palms have been planted, forming an paradisal landscape that is unmissable for anyone who wants to grasp the essence of Gran Canaria. Surrounded by banana trees which supply fruit to all of Spain, the garden envelops you in its velvety air and sweet scents, carrying you back to the Golden Age.

Above The porch has a tropical air.

Following pages Bird of paradise (*Strelitzia reginae*) flowers with an evocative shroud of cobwebs.

45

JARDÍN DE CACTUS

Gautiza, Lanzarote

Among the rivers of lava that form the mysterious landscapes of Lanzarote, you find the utterly original Cactus Garden, the last of the works created by César Manrique (1919–92) on his native island,* all of which were intended to celebrate this extraordinary environment. 'Lanzarote is pure magic . . . a clear beauty, naked and insolent. A constant education. This unknown and profound environment is somehow aware of the great spectacle it offers,' remarked this multifaceted artist. Linked to the informalist movement of abstract art, after twenty hectic years in Madrid and three in New York, Manrique returned to Lanzarote for good in 1966. He immediately set about salvaging what he could of the island's natural and cultural landscape. It would be impossible to conceive of Lanzarote as it is today without his pioneering work in sustainable tourism.

Opened in 1990, the Cactus Garden combines art, architecture and landscape in a way that is typical of its creator, using the language of contemporary art to fuse traditional and local elements. Indivisible from their settings, Manrique called these works 'art-nature/nature-art', reflecting

Countless species of cacti and succulents provide a multitude of shapes and colours against the volcanic soil.

on the relationship between man and his environment.

The choice of location is deliberate, as it is in the heart of the region where prickly pears are cultivated. These were previously a major source of income for the island, as parasitic beetles were harvested from the plants to create carmine, a valuable natural dye. Manrique placed the garden amid a sea of cactus, in an abandoned quarry, thinking to renew this degraded land. The quarry had previously been a source of the volcanic sand known as lapillo, used in local horticulture and in the garden itself to maintain soil humidity.

Semicircular in form, the garden is a natural amphitheatre, with a cast of more than 10,000 plants of almost 1,000 different species. Most are from the cactus family and originate in the Americas, while the indigenous flora of the Canary Islands is represented by euphorbias and succulents, including *Aeonium lancerottense*, endemic to Lanzarote.

These bizarre sculptural plants, experts in hoarding water, are perfectly suited to the desert surroundings, where the soil is stony and rain scarce. Many flower spectacularly but briefly.

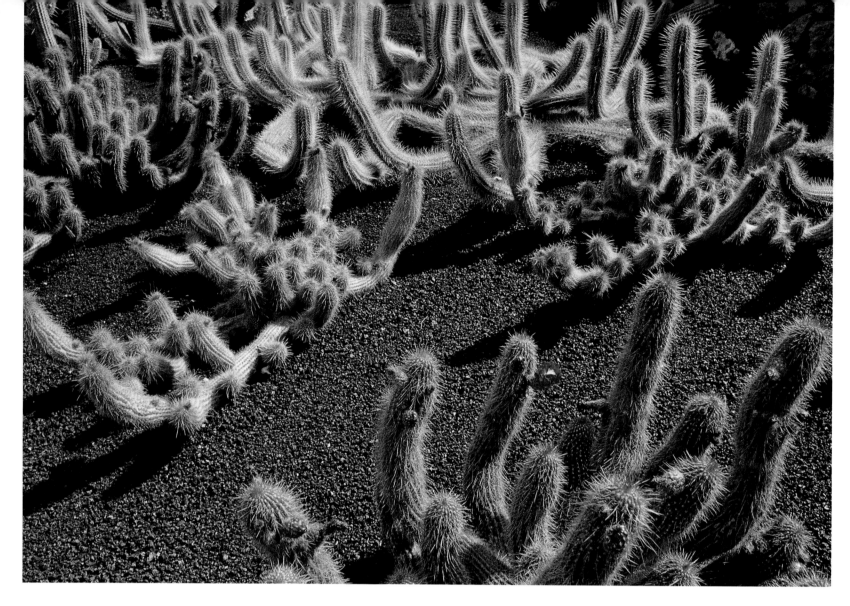

The blooms of *Selenicereus inermis*, for example, last for only a few hours in the middle of the night: hence the plant's common name of moonlight cactus.

The terraces recall the island's traditional farming methods. From them you can admire the spectacular scene, which is dominated by monoliths of petrified lava, remnants of the quarrying operation preserved and converted into sculptures.

This is a complete work, in that Manrique designed everything from the interior of the café to the giant metal cactus which directs passing traffic to the garden. Nature is also present in every detail: it was the basic reference for Manrique's art and life. 'The delight I take in living and in constant creation springs from my study, contemplation and love for the great wisdom of the natural world.' *Manrique's other works on Lanzarote are El Mirador del Rio, Jameos de Agua, Casa-Museo del Campesino, the restaurant Diablo, La Ruta de los Volcanes in Timanfaya, El Castillo de San José and his own home, which now houses the César Manrique Foundation.*

Above and right The plants are like living sculptures.

Opposite Among the astonishing shapes are these *Echinocactus* or mother-in-law's seat.

Mediterranean

JARDINES ARTIGAS

La Pobla de Lillet, Cataluña

Like everything he made, these gardens by the great architect Antonio Gaudí spring from his profound love and knowledge of nature. Regarding himself not as a creator but rather as a mere interpreter of creation, he said, 'Originality consists of returning to the origin. A work is original in so far as it returns to the simplicity of the very first solutions.' Following this humble idea of the artist as a propagator of natural laws, Gaudí was able to grasp the savage beauty of the gorge which contains the Artigas Gardens by using rough local stones to highlight its dramatic features. Divided by the river Llobregat, which rises among the stones and trees at their base, the steep slopes are linked by rustic bridges which seem to be extensions of their surroundings.

Gaudí first visited the Pyrenean town La Pobla de Lillet in 1902 to inspect work on the nearby Chalet de Catllaràs, a lodging for mining engineers commissioned by Eusebio Güell. The fabric manufacturer Joan Artigas i Alart, impressed by Gaudí's work on Park Güell in Barcelona (see page 58), asked him to design a garden on a plot behind his textile factory.

A magnificent view from La Glorieta, a point where the garden blends with the surrounding landscape.

Right Two snakes watch over the original entrance to the garden.

Below Made of reinforced concrete and local stone, two statues of human figures with gardening baskets stand out on the Puente de los Arcos (Bridge of Arches).

Gaudí sketched an outline for what was to be the one garden-only work in his career, and the next year he sent construction workers from Park Güell to begin making it. After a few months they had built a grotto with large unworked stones to protect the source of the medicinal water which gave the garden its original name of Fuente de La Magnesia (the Magnesia Spring). This was to be the only part of the garden seen by Joan Artigas i Alart, who died later that year. His son Joan Artigas i Casas continued the project with local builders who had worked with the men from Park Güell. But during the Spanish Civil War of 1936–9 the Artigas factory was destroyed and the family moved to Barcelona. Because of its remote location the garden was then utterly forgotten.

It was not until 1992, after exhaustive research, that the gardens were restored under the auspices of the Real Cátedra Gaudí, which is dedicated to the study and conservation of Gaudí's work. This unknown treasure of landscape design was returned to its former glory, the restoration including sculptures by Ramón Millet i Domènech from Gaudí's original designs.

Although clearly a product of the same unique creative temperament as the gardens at Park Güell, the garden contains notable differences, as this most delightful of architects never used the same solution more than once, and always took pains to connect his work to its immediate surroundings. In contrast to the bright mosaics of Barcelona – which would

not have survived the harsh winters in La Pobla de Lillet – the Artigas Gardens are characterized by the use of local stone, which contrasts with the green of the native plants. While Park Güell is a dry garden, this is a wet one, with the river at its heart, defining the space with bridges, balconies and viewpoints of stone and reinforced concrete. It is hard to miss the extraordinary planters on the Puente de los Arcos (the Bridge of Arches), whose human forms – one male, one female – recall the caryatid in Park Güell.

One constant in Gaudi's work is the use of religious symbols, and this garden is no exception. Four stone sculptures represent the four evangelists: the eagle overlooking the square for St John, an ox fountain in the pine grove for St Luke, a lion fountain near the pergola for St Mark and an angel representing St Matthew, which appears to have originally stood next to the stone cascade. A bird's-eye view of the garden would reveal that the four evangelists form the shape of the Cross. The bridge, originally conceived as the only way in and out of the garden, is guarded by planters in the form of snakes, the mythical protectors of sacred places and priceless treasure.

Left An eagle guards the bridge over the river Llobregat which leads to the upper garden.

Above Imitating wood, this rustic fence contributes to the blend of nature and architecture.

PARK GÜELL

Barcelona

'The greatest book of all is the book of Nature, forever open and forever worth reading. Every other book is a version of this one, riddled with the errors and interpolations of man,' declared Antonio Gaudí, creator of one of the most striking, uncategorizable gardens in the world, Park Güell. Nature was the guiding light for this Catalan architect; in nature the divine creation was written and there God abided still. Profoundly religious, Gaudí viewed the re-creation of natural forms and structures as steps in a spiritual pilgrimage, whose destination was a marriage of nature and architecture, a new Eden where man could once again meet God.

Park Güell, built between 1900 and 1914, was conceived by Gaudí's extraordinarily rich and cultured patron Eusebio Güell as a garden city along British or American lines (hence the use of the English word 'park'). It was to be an ideal community, on a mountainous hillside close to Barcelona, but not part of it; an exclusive estate of 15 hectares divided into sixty roughly triangular plots, adapted to the terrain. Those buying the plots would sign contracts prohibiting the felling of trees, and stipulating, for instance, that the house should cover no more than

The great serpentine bench winding round the edge of the Greek Theatre is an imaginative collage of ceramic fragments known as *trencadís*, Park Güell's defining feature.

one-sixth of the plot, and that garden fences should be no more than 80 centimetres high. More than half of the estate would be dedicated to green space, to promote 'beauty, recreation, health and hygiene'. This Arcadian project was to prove an economic disaster, however. Only two houses were built – one for Gaudí and one for the lawyer Trías – not including the Güell residence, which was located in

the original manor house on the estate. What is today the Gaudí Museum was built as a prototype by Francisco Berenguer. It remained unsold until finally occupied by Gaudí himself.

The first challenge the architect faced was in linking the plots and communal spaces over the very uneven terrain. Preferring not to level the ground, he designed a series of winding paths with arcades whose

Left Porticoes clad in local stone blend with the terrain.

Top Zoomorphic shapes at the entrance to the carriage park bring elephants to mind.

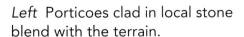

Above left Agaves crown these primitive columns.

Below left Leaning columns support a viaduct.

angled columns were clad in local stone to integrate them with the surrounding landscape and preserve the essence of the place. Agaves were planted at the top of buttresses in the form of palm trees. The upper level was intended for carriages and motor vehicles, while the lower colonnade was for pedestrians. As elsewhere in the park, viaducts covered with shrubs and a tapestry of hanging and climbing plants harmonize with the natural setting: an imitation, a representation and a symbol of nature.

The site of the park was known as Montaña Pelada, or Bare Mountain, and the scarce vegetation was limited to scrub and a few carob trees. Sympathetic to the natural surroundings, Gaudí planted drought-tolerant Mediterranean species including pine, ilex and palm (*Phoenix dactylifera*). It could be said without exaggeration that Park Güell is a natural garden *avant le mot* as well as being an environmentally friendly and sustainable development.

Far left The English word 'park' is used for this garden.

Left The ceramic covering of this gatehouse tower almost looks like scales.

At the same time, Gaudí anticipated by almost a century the current explosion of interest in recycling. He bound fragments of glazed tiles and discarded crockery with mortar to create the mosaics known as *trencadís*. Dressing his favoured organic forms in this brightly coloured second skin, he was able to conjure a fantastical world. The dazzling effect he achieved is evident even in the gatehouses that welcome visitors to the park. Like fairytale gingerbread houses, the porter's lodge stands to the right of the entrance and the visitors' waiting room on the left. Here is Gaudí's singular world, full of references and symbols, zoomorphic shapes, mushroom-shaped chimneys and – at the top of the highest tower – a great cross. Both Gaudí and Güell were fervent Catholics and envisioned a church at the summit of the mountain. This remained unbuilt and the spot today is known as Calvary.

A great flight of steps with a succession of sculptural fountains leads from the entrance to the central square. The first fountain is in the form of a grotto, and the second is the yellow and red Catalan crest with a dragon's head. The third is the

Above left and right Details of the main flight of steps: the park's emblematic salamander and the shield of Catalonia with a dragon spouting water.

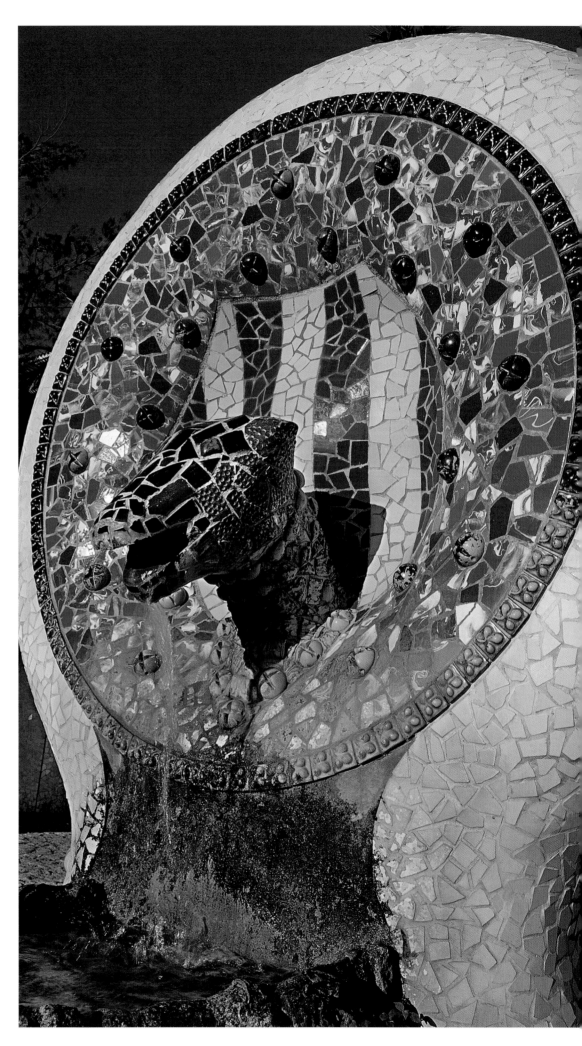

spectacular multicoloured salamander that has come to symbolize the garden. Given the complex symbolism of Gaudí's work, this could refer to the alchemical salamander, representing the element of fire; or it could be emblematic of the French city of Nîmes, where Güell studied; or it could perhaps be a dragon guarding the entrance to the park. At the final turn of the steps is a curiously shaped bench, deftly positioned to catch the sun in winter and the shade in summer.

At the top of the steps is an impressive covered space, supported by eighty-six Doric columns, known as El Templo (the Temple) or La Sala Hipóstila (the Hypostyle Hall). This was originally conceived as a covered market that would operate twice weekly for residents. For the sake of hygiene the lower part of the columns was covered with white *trencadís*, while the roof is adorned with wonderful circular compositions by the architect Josep María Pujol, under Gaudí's direction. The seasons

are represented in four large rosettes, made out of fragments of porcelain, crockery and glass, while fourteen smaller rosettes chart the phases of the moon.

Gaudí's ingenuity as an architect is also much in evidence: above this hall is the open space known as the Greek Theatre, where rainwater collects and flows through the hollow interiors of the columns to an enormous cistern under the floor, to supply the houses that were to come. Excess water flows to the three fountains on the main steps.

The Greek Theatre was to be the community's main public space. Here is the famous undulating bench, which follows the curving shape of the temple while suggesting at the same time the waves of the nearby Mediterranean. To make sure the bench was as accommodating as possible, Gaudí experimented with one of the young construction workers to find the most comfortable seating design. In decorating the bench Gaudí, with Pujol, raised the technique of *trencadís* to great art, creating a masterpiece whose astonishing abstract combinations of form and colour anticipate the collages of more recent art. Sunlight glancing on the ceramic surface sometimes has the effect of animating the bench, transforming it into a giant serpent, denizen of the extraordinary world created by this towering genius of world architecture.

Park Güell became a public park in 1923 and is now one of Spain's greatest attractions, welcoming over four million visitors every year.

Above left and right Doric columns in the Temple support the Greek Theatre above and channel rainwater into an underground cistern. The magnificent ceiling roses are made of fragments of porcelain, glass and china.

LABERINTO DE HORTA

'You can get out without making a detour; the maze is simple. No need for the yarn Ariadne gave to Theseus.' This is the invitation inscribed at the entrance to the maze at Horta, alluding to the story of the Minotaur in which Ariadne's gift of a ball of thread to Theseus allows him to retrace his route after killing the beast. In this eighteenth-century neoclassical garden, the labyrinth is not the place of terror it was in ancient Greece but an amusing puzzle, perfect for a game of hide and seek. In the middle of the maze, instead of the monster of Knossos there is a statue of Eros, representing earthly love.

Classical style and mythological allusions are so central to the garden's design that the whole place is named after its heart and soul: the maze

Left A view of the maze, with clipped box hedges in the foreground. Water is everywhere in this garden.

Above Cypress (*Cupressus sempervirens*) hedges form the old walls of the maze. The sound of water indicates the way out.

of tall clipped cypress hedges. This was begun in 1791 by the owner, Juan Antonio Desvalls, Marquis of Llupià and Alfarràs, a connoisseur and intellectual who worked with the Italian architect Domenico Bugatti and the French gardener Delvalet, choosing a spot close to Barcelona, where fresh air and abundant water made it the perfect setting for a country house.

The first part of the garden to be completed was the pool at the upper end, which serves as a reservoir for the irrigation system. While this is typical of the Hispano-Islamic tradition of garden design, with its references to classical antiquity the maze also reflects the sophisticated ambience of the time of its creation.

Beyond the maze, the three distinct levels of the garden are best appreciated in ascending order. The steps, balustrades and numerous classical sculptures speak of the design's Italian origins. A magnificent flight of steps leads to the second level, where circular temples overlook the maze, while in the upper part a neoclassical pavilion is reflected in a tank. Behind this, a nymph reclines in a grotto, very like one at the iconic

A small space on the lower level with clipped box hedges invites the visitor to go up the steps and discover the garden at the top.

English landscape garden Stourhead, as the Marquesa de Casa Valdés points out in her book on Spanish gardens.

A romantic garden added in the mid-nineteenth century adds a different mood. While the precision and clarity of the neoclassical garden invite an intellectual response, this shady place, full of asymmetry and irregularity, is designed to play on the emotions. A picturesque cemetery, hermitage and artificial waterfall complete the scene.

This magnificent garden museum passed to the city of Barcelona in 1968. Until then, it belonged to the descendants of Antonio Desvalls. For almost two centuries it was an enviable summer retreat, the scene of family reunions and festive occasions and a setting for open-air theatre. When Charles IV attended one of these extravagant celebrations in 1802, he commented to the owner that the gardens were really too much for just one man. The marquis's astute reply was that unfortunately they were really too little to offer to one's king. No doubt he had in mind the fate of the French Minister of Finance Fouquet, who spent the rest of his life in prison after inviting Louis XIV to a spectacular reception at his garden of Vaux-le-Vicomte and finding that the king could not bear to be outdone.

An elegant neoclassical pavilion on the upper terrace, next to the tank which stores the garden's water supply, with *Agapanthus africanus* in the foreground.

PARQUE SAMÁ
Cambrils, Cataluña

'Alice opened the door and found that it led into a small passage, not much larger than a rat-hole: she knelt down and looked along a passage into the loveliest garden you ever saw.'

The fantastic scene Alice glimpses in Lewis Carroll's *Alice's Adventures in Wonderland* could almost be the extravagant, dreamlike Parque Samá. But, unlike Alice, the visitor does not need to drink magic potions or take strange pills to get into this fairytale garden.

One of Spain's oddities, the park is the creation of Salvador Samá i Torrents, the Marquis of Marianao, whose father amassed a huge fortune in Cuba. In 1881 Salvador commissioned a colonial-style mansion and a walled park, to occupy 14 hectares of flat land among fields of vines and fruit trees. The architect, Josep Fontseré i Mestre, was also responsible for the Parque de la Ciudadela in Barcelona. He employed the young Antonio Gaudí as a draftsman in his office and the young man may have been involved with the work on the park.

The heart of this strange world is undoubtedly the huge ornamental lake with its three islets of limestone bound with cement, an apotheosis of the late nineteenth-century fashion for ornamental rockery. The scale of the work is enormous: the lake covers more than a hectare and is 3 metres deep. An impressive swamp cypress (*Taxodium distichum*) grows on the smallest of the islets, its trailing roots providing an ideal home for the turtles that thrive in the lake. The central

Above left and right These three islets in a hectare of lake are a fantasy of ornamental rockwork.

island has a hollow mountain with a mooring underneath and a bandstand on the summit, where in bygone days an orchestra would play at teatime.

A channel runs beween the lake and the waterfall, which is fed through a subterranean tunnel over 5 kilometres long. The water is also used for irrigation, and it would not be possible to support the exuberant plants without it. There is a collection of palms (*Phoenix canariensis*, *P. dactilifera* and *P. roebeleni*, *Washingtonia robusta* and *W. filifera*, *Chamaerops excelsa* and *C. humilis*) mixed with pine, cedar, eucalyptus and plane trees. Paths wind between flower beds covered by ivy, which also cloaks the trunks of the trees, giving the whole park a junglelike atmosphere.

Everywhere there are strange animal enclosures, built in the same rockwork style as the rest of the garden ornaments. These are vestiges of Samá's private menagerie, which included monkeys, panthers, lions and crocodiles. These disappeared during the Civil War of 1936–9 and today only a few peacocks, parrots, ducks and turtles inhabit the garden.

Above The view from the back of the house, with an iron fountain and fine specimens of Canary Island date palm.

Right Parque Samá is home to an extraordinary collection of palm trees.

Far right The old parrot house.

Opposite Water cascades into the lake.

Following pages Ivy-covered steps lead to a Caribbean-style terrace.

JARDÍN DE MONTFORTE

Valencia

Amid the identikit developments which sprawl around Valencia, where once there were fields and gardens, the survival of the garden at Montforte is something of a miracle. It is the epitome of what the Romans called *locus amoenus*, an earthly paradise, utopian and unreal, set apart from the everyday world – a place where time stands still.

Dating from 1849, the house and garden were developed on farmland by the Valencian architect Sebastián Monleón at the request of the industrialist J.B. Romero, later the Marquis of San Juan. The estate acquired its current name some decades later when it passed to a niece who had married into the Montforte family.

Many artists have been captivated by the garden's beauty, among them Santiago Rusiñol, who described it as 'small, secluded and peaceful. Marble busts stand before the cypresses, statues emerge from box hedges. There are myrtle arches, jets of water, willows, moss . . . and symmetry. A classical garden made romantic by time!'

In fact, both styles are present in the garden's design: a more formal,

Clipped hedges of euonymus give structure to a parterre centred on a statue personifying Asia. An inviting tunnel of bougainvillea runs around the garden wall in the background.

architectural style based on cypresses and clipped hedges, and another looser style in the landscape tradition. The garden is a series of outdoor rooms. Closer to the house, these are more formally defined by walls of cypress, while further away there are mysterious shady corners: a large pool, a wooded area and an artificial hill concealing a water tank.

Carefully restored in the 1940s, the garden passed into public ownership in the 1970s, when the parterres by the current entrance were added.

Another striking feature is the collection of Carrara marble statues, whose smooth white figures contrast with the green of the architectural planting. Busts of philosophers and mythological characters tell the garden's story. Ceres, the goddess of agriculture and the fruits of the earth, and Flora, the goddess of flowers and trees, represent the transformation of farmland into garden. The presence of the shepherd Daphnis and the nymph Chloe emphasize that this is an idyllic world, a bower of bliss, far from the mundane mediocrity of what lies beyond.

Left A composition of green hedges, rose bushes and bougainvillea in the formal garden.

Right, above and below Architectural and sculptural elements, including the gods Bacchus and Mercury on either side of the portal, lend this corner of the garden a classical flavour.

Following pages Detail of the new garden laid out in 1971 with euonymus hedges marking out a sea of *Hydrangea macrophylla*.

HUERTO DEL CURA
Elche, Valencia

'And the Lord God planted a garden in Eden . . .' The biblical Eden would have been an oasis in the desert: a frondy refuge of peaceful shade in the middle of arid, hostile surroundings. In the centre of this first enclosed garden – a *hortus conclusus* – was the Tree of Life, which would probably have been a date palm (*Phoenix dactylifera*). It is this tree that defines the main character of the Palmeral de Elche, the astonishing palm groves that contain the Huerto del Cura.

'I imagined myself transported to the plains of Alexandria or mighty Cairo,' the French traveller Jean François Peyron wrote in his *Essais sur l'Espagne: Voyage fait en Espagne en 1777 et 1778* of this unique and surprising place. It contains the greatest concentration of palm trees in Europe, today covering more than 500 hectares and consisting of more than 200,000 specimens. With origins that can be traced back more than 2,500 years to the Phoenician traders who brought the first palm trees to Spain, the Palmeral owes its current form to the Arabs, who developed it from the eighth century onwards. Masters in exploiting whatever scarce water was available in desert lands, they created a complex network of irrigation channels – still in use today – and planted palm trees along them, bordering parcels of productive land.

El Huerto del Cura, the Priest's Plot, was originally one of these cultivated areas, whose high canopy of palm leaves created a microclimate that allowed fruits, cereals and vegetables to be grown. The priest Andrés Castaño grew up there in the second half of the nineteenth century. He became the owner in 1900, and the place is named after him. The *huerto* became a tourist attraction through his habit of dedicating each tree to a different public figure or, as he put it, 'baptizing the palms'. After the priest's death, the *huerto* passed into the hands of its current owners, the Orts family, who began to transform it into a garden in the 1940s. Retaining the structure of the *huerto* with its lines of palms, they formed new paths and pools while at the same time planting a great variety of new species, including the cactus collection and the bamboo grove.

But the star of the *huerto* is without question the Palmera Imperial, a huge date palm in the shape of

Opposite Lines of palm trees recall the original structure of the palm groves, next to the benches made of palm tree trunks. To the left is a bust of the Empress Elisabeth of Austria.

Far left The spectacular 160-year-old specimen of *Phoenix dactylifera* known as the Imperial Palm, which was named in honour of the Empress Elisabeth.

Left Agaves and groups of *Yucca elephantipes*.

a candelabra, which was dedicated to the Empress Elizabeth of Austria, 'Sissi', following a visit from her. This 'Prince of the Vegetable Kingdom', as Linnaeus called it, despite its great size is not strictly a tree but a shrub. It was also one of the first plants to be cultivated by man, and is put to many uses: the dates are eaten, the stones are fed to animals and the leaves are used for baskets, hats, brooms – or, as happens at Elche, as religious objects in the ceremonies of Holy Week.

The date palm was a sacred tree in antiquity; in Egypt it symbolized eternity and fertility, while in Rome it was the symbol of victory, ever present on Palm Sunday as a symbol of Christ's victory over death. Its Latin genus name *Phoenix* is an allusion to that mythological bird that rises from the ashes, as the palm similarly seems to sprout miraculously from nothing. It is the quintessence of creation.

The peacock's striking beauty has found a place in the gardens of the East and West since time immemorial.

RAIXA
Buñola, Mallorca

The Proustian phrase which echoes through the Spanish film *Bearn o la sala de las muñecas*, shot here at Raixa – 'The true paradises are the paradises that we have lost' – is apt for this romantic, faded place, whose every corner is loaded with nostalgia for bygone days.

A witness to the swings in fortune of Mallorca and its most powerful dynasties, this Italianate garden makes the most of its setting in the foothills of the Sierra de la Tramontana, looking out over the bay of Palma. In its current form it was largely laid out in the late eighteenth and early nineteenth centuries by Cardinal Antonio Despuig i Dameto.

Like many other Mallorcan estates or *sones*, Raixa dates from the Islamic period, when it was a farm. On conquering the island in the thirteenth century, the Christian King Jaime I granted the estate to the Count of Ampurias in recognition of his support. It was acquired by the 1st Count of Montenegro in 1660, and it stayed in

Above A neo-Moorish lookout in the romantic garden.

Right and opposite The enormous water tank reflects the trees. Meals were served on the terrace to the right.

his family until their ruin in the early twentieth century. Since 2002 it has belonged to the Spanish Department of the Environment and the local government of Mallorca.

Cardinal Antonio Despuig i Dameto was the son of the 3rd Count of Montenegro. He transformed the ancient grange into a spectacular country house, following models he had observed in Italy, where he had spent much of his life. A patron of the arts and a keen antiquarian, he had an archaeological collection that included pieces from his excavations near Rome. Today these treasures are kept in Palma's Historical Museum at Castillo de Bellver. In 1802 the cardinal engaged the Italian architect Giovanni Lazzarini to make an ambitious design, which appears never to have been carried out.

As noted by the Marquesa de Casa Valdés, the learned cardinal was also interested in botany, and through his connections at the Botanical Gardens in Madrid he assembled a collection of exotic plants from the Americas. None of these plants remains in the garden today, which is a combination of the cardinal's neoclassical outline and later nineteenth-century additions including a picturesque belvedere.

The garden divides in two: the lower half in front of the house and the upper on the hillside to the rear, dominated by the flight of steps that is the garden's most striking feature. The steps rise in seven flights to a statue of Apollo at the top, as though the god of light and the sun had simply descended from Mount Parnassus with his Muses. Everything here, from the mature cypresses to the abundance of sculpture, is redolent of Mediterranean antiquity. Water flows from the mountain into channels and fountains to freshen the air. The garden's other emblematic feature is a beautiful pool, originally a water tank for irrigation. This is reached by a path off one of the terraces, where another flight of stairs leads to a platform with chairs. The Marquesa de Casa Valdés also observed that the cardinal furnished this outdoor room with a stone table, to emulate the alfresco dining so enjoyed by Cardinal Gambara at Villa Lante in Italy in the previous century.

Descending in terraces marked by four arches of clipped cypress, the lower gardens lie in front of the Italianate loggia, an external gallery which is also typical of Mallorcan *sones*. Mature cypress, monkey puzzle, palm and orange trees soften the sharp lines of the original design, but this is precisely the source of Raixa's considerable charm. Santiago Rusiñol, whose oil paintings immortalize the garden, wrote that 'the old gardens are dying, but they die in such a noble fashion that a new poetry is born, the poetry of great declines.'

Opposite The monumental staircase rises in seven flights behind the house.

Above left A terracotta mask.

Below left Decorative and sculptural elements in abundance transport the visitor to Italy.

ALFABIA
Buñola, Mallorca

'If you can stand paradise then go to Mallorca,' the writer Gertrude Stein told her English friend Robert Graves, and he ended up spending a great part of his life on the island. In Alfabia, whose origins stretch back to the Moorish period, it is possible to catch a glimpse of this earthly Eden. Despite later modifications, this evocative place is essentially faithful to the Islamic ideal of the garden orchard as a metaphor of paradise. Ornamental planting combines with groves of fruit trees, wide horizons alternate with enclosed spaces, and water abounds in all its forms.

The garden owes its abundance of water, channelled in *acequias* (the Spanish word for irrigation channels, derived from the Arabic *sakiya*) and collected in a beautiful pool, to its position at the foot of the Sierra de Alfabia, north of the island's capital, Palma. It is said to have been given to the Moorish noble Ben Abet, in recognition of support for the Christian King Jaime I of Aragon during his conquest of the island in 1229. At the entry to the patio a wooden ceiling dating from the twelfth century retains something of this period, with the inscription 'Allah is great. Allah is all-mighty. There is no God but Allah.'

The sensational pergola, where fine sprays of water shoot across from both sides.

Left A majestic plane tree in the front courtyard.

Right The artificial lake, ringed with palms and bamboo.

Below The romantic garden behind the house. In the foreground, a Swiss cheese plant (*Monstera deliciosa*) and *Chamaerops humilis.*

The patio itself is a typical Mallorcan *clastra*, dominated by a massive plane tree.

Alfabia as it appears today was predominantly shaped by its mid-eighteenth-century owner Gabriel de Berga y Zaforteza. Baroque façades were added to the medieval walls and various classical architectural details to the property. The sensational pergola that is the garden's highlight belongs to this period. Clad in ivy, it is a fine example of *giochi d'acqua*, the water tricks which characterize Italian Renaissance gardens and which remained popular throughout Europe in the following centuries. At the end of the pergola, fine jets of water shoot from both sides to drench the unwary visitor – a refreshing experience on a hot summer day. These jets are fed by a great vaulted tank, where a glance through the porthole with the vegetation in the background transports the visitor to a strange imaginary world.

An impressive flight of steps flanked by palm trees and water channels is a fusion of Hispano-Islamic and Italian styles, while the garden to the rear of the house has a quite different character. Laid out in the nineteenth century in the English landscape tradition, this has a large artificial pond, winding paths and a shady atmosphere created by a dense planting of bamboo, palm and eucalyptus. The perfect refuge, it is one of those places Yeats described as 'gardens where a soul's at ease'.

Following pages Steps lined with agaves and palms lead into the gardens from the patio at the entrance.

PEDRERES DE S'HOSTAL
Ciudadela, Menorca

A visit to the gardens in these ancient quarries outside Ciudadela in Menorca is an amazing journey to the centre of the earth, to a fantastical terrain of mysterious paths and dreamscapes.

'It's the landscape's sculpted body,' remarks the French sculptor Laetitia Sauleau, the presiding spirit of these spellbinding gardens. In 1994, fascinated by the ancient Menorcan sandstone quarries, she set up the association Líthica to prevent them from being turned into a rubbish dump, and to preserve them as an art space in which to explore the relationship between man and stone, the geological and the ecological.

There is a long history of sunken gardens in Menorca. 'When a quarry was exhausted, it was used to grow fruit, vines and vegetables, sheltered from the wind,' explains José Bravo, who has set up a plantation in the middle of the old quarry. This network of enclosed gardens, whose rugged stone walls were worked by hand, features a typically Mediterranean range of fruit and vegetables, as well as some local specialities such as carob trees, sumac, rosemary and chamomile. Sunk deep in the belly of the earth, these spaces are pregnant with silence.

Following the winding path that connects the different spaces, you suddenly come upon a small opening in the rock. Squeeze through and you are astonished to find an exquisite cloistered garden, whose central fountain bears the inscription 'Approach, you who thirst. If the waves fail you, the Goddess will provide eternal water.' Old-fashioned roses and medicinal herbs complete the sensation of having come upon a symbolic garden, a metaphor for a lost paradise.

The older quarries, shaped by hand and chisel, have a human scale, intimate and sheltering. The more recent excavations, dug by machine, are another world. Monochrome and abstract, these huge spaces are like giant conceptual works of art. They make a perfect setting for many of the events organized by Líthica: concerts, parties, sculpture workshops, even Tai Chi classes.

Here we also find a stone maze, one of the world's most ancient and enigmatic symbols. I suspect that, in fact, the whole place is a maze, a rite of passage leading to the heart of the earth. Or as Laetitia puts it, 'It's an imaginative journey, when your mind is constantly surprised by evocations of lost civilizations or simply stunned by the power of these great eroded rocks, and you want to turn yourself into the vine clinging to the rock, or to the earth gilding it.'

Left Of medieval inspiration, the central fountain in this garden orchard is flanked by *Rosa gallica* and *R.* x *alba* 'Alba Maxima'.

Above A maze in one of the quarries excavated by machines.

Following pages The fascinating abstract forms of the vertical walls were created without any aesthetic intent.

The
Centre

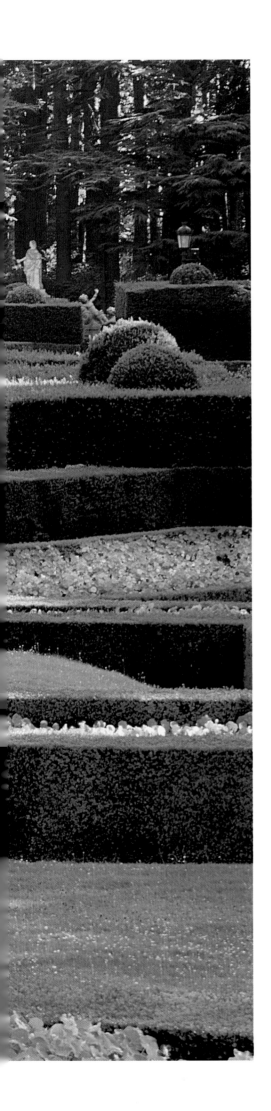

PALACIO REAL DE LA GRANJA DE SAN ILDELFONSO

Castilla y León, Segovia

'Your first duty is to be a good Spaniard. But do not forget that you are French by birth.' These were the words of the Sun King, Louis XIV, to his grandson, the Duke of Anjou, as he set off to assume the Spanish throne as Philip V. These words take shape in the magnificent gardens at La Granja, where, despite a number of Spanish features, a French heart beats to the rhythm of the splendid court where Philip spent the first seventeen years of his life.

The king discovered this alpine spot in 1718 when out hunting, and immediately fell in love with its endless pine groves and abundant springs of crystal water. It was a perfect escape from the arid Castilian plain, so alien to a young man raised among France's rolling green landscapes. At the time all that stood here was a monastic lodge belonging to the Hieronymite order, and a medieval hermitage dedicated to St Ildelfonso.

Above The parterre in front of the main façade, with box hedges and roses.

Left The Parterre de la Fama: box and yew hedges alongside the omnipresent mythological sculptures, with the Fuente de Fama (Fountain of Fame) in the background.

Hounded by depression, Philip was planning – despite his youth – to renounce the Spanish throne, and was looking for a place to retire. With this in mind, he began work in 1720 on the palace and gardens of La Granja de San Ildelfonso. Three years later, the king's private apartments were complete, and in January 1724 Philip handed power to his son, Louis I. However, his much-anticipated retirement was brief: his successor died six months later, and Philip returned to reign until his death in 1746. The change of plan affected La Granja too: originally intended as a refuge, from that moment on it became the residence of the ruler and his court.

The gardens were developed from an original design by René Carlier, which drew inspiration from the French Château de Marly, later destroyed in the Revolution. At Carlier's death in 1722 direction of the project passed to Esteban Boutelou and Esteban Marchand. There is a strong French character to the expansive design, based on clearly defined axes and a rigorous sense of order, though the abstract perspectives are interrupted by the surrounding mountains.

Left The Fuente de Fama's 50-metre-high jet is thought to be the highest in Europe.

Right Forming a principal axis of the garden, this succession of pools with fountains known as the Carrera de Caballos (Horse Race) recalls the gardens at Versailles.

Below Small copses bordered by hornbeam hedges, in the French style.

The gardens are effectively a series of verdant settings for a seemingly endless array of spectacular sculptures by French artists who had worked at Marly. To save time and money, almost all the pieces were cast in lead and then coated to imitate bronze and gold. With their asymmetrical forms, undulating lines and mythological themes, the sculptures are archetypally rococo in style.

The highlights of these gardens are the fountains, which still astonish visitors today. To generate the necessary water pressure, they are fed by a great artificial lake known as El Mar (The Sea), on the garden's upper level. The jet of the Fuente de Fama (Fountain of Fame) is reputed to be the highest in Europe, erupting 50 metres from the trumpet of the goddess Fame to proclaim the glory of the Spanish throne. The king and his second wife, Isabel de Farnesio, were keen hunters, and the statue of the goddess Diana, the huntress, in the spectacular Fuente de los Baños de Diana, is perhaps in homage to the queen. This was the last fountain to be completed before the death of the king, who when he saw it working for the first time remarked 'It cost three million and amused me for three minutes.' It was inspired by a design at the French court, as was the row of fountains known as La Carrera de Caballos (Horse Race), whose splendid ascending perspective owes an obvious debt to the Grand Canal at Versailles.

The Gallic influence is also found in the clipped hedges of hornbeam (*Carpinus betulus*) and yew (*Taxus baccata*), two species brought from France and used here for the first time in Spain. Despite the gardens'

unmistakably French character, various elements derive from the Spanish tradition, with its Hispano-Islamic roots: the absence of long views, the positioning of the main water supply in the upper part of the garden and the open irrigation channels.

A physic garden supplied medicinal plants to the royal pharmacy, and in the Queen's Garden Isabel's Italian gardeners encouraged fruit trees to adapt to the severe Castilian climate. After her husband's death the queen turned La Granja into a permanent residence, saying that in winter it became a *pastel de nieves*, an ice cake. Because of its cool climate, La Granja was the summer residence of the Spanish royal family through to the first decades of the twentieth century.

Above A marble cascade runs along the main axis, with the Sierra de Guadarrama in the distance.

Right The physic garden with a sumac (*Rhus coriaria*) in the foreground.

Following pages The main parterre under one of winter's frequent snowfalls.

The nineteenth century saw the introduction of new species, including huge sequoias and cedars, which have little in common with the garden's original spirit. The eighteenth-century hornbeam maze has recently been restored. Originally the scene of romantic intrigues among the idle courtiers, today it is a beguiling spot in which it is hard to resist

the pleasure of losing oneself.

La Granja is the masterpiece of the man who would rather not be king, who despite his melancholy left as his legacy this joyful garden of his boyhood, and whose spectacular fountains and refreshing shade bring to mind the Spanish saying 'childhood is the patio we play on for the rest of our lives'.

EL ROMERAL DE SAN MARCOS

Segovia, Castilla y León

'With this project I have almost unconsciously had the desire to evoke the Hispano-Islamic gardens I encountered when I arrived in Spain. The terraces, the stream of water, the water tanks, the contrast of light and shadow and planting which reveals my preference for cypress, box, myrtle and rose have all combined to bring my intended design to fruition,' said the landscape architect Leandro Silva (1930–2000) of his most personal work – his own garden – which evolved over thirty years by the river Eresma, at the foot of the monumental city of Segovia.

The garden, completely independent of the house, extends over half a hectare, and is arranged in terraces that preserve the terrain's

Above A wintry view of the stepped path and its central rill, flanked by yew.

Right The octagonal cistern surrounded by rose of Sharon (*Hypericum calycinum*) is the heart of the garden.

steep slope and create a labyrinthine, secluded and elusive space. Deployed along a winding path, with countless steps, small garden rooms invite the visitor to pause, to linger and to contemplate the magnificent landscape and the silhouette of Segovia's *alcazar*, its castle. On the other side, the garden is sheltered from the cold north wind by dramatic limestone rocks. Revealing its Hispano-Islamic roots, the whole garden is a treat for the senses. Scented plants delight the nose, the textures of the ground invite touch, birdsong caresses the ear, ripe fruits beguile the tongue and the planting's chromatic play amazes the eye.

'One of the nice things we discovered about the place was the abundance of water. You can hear it springing from the limestone, and it was collected in tanks long before we arrived. This inspired me to make more water tanks, and linking them with long channels became a feature of the garden's design,' Silva explained. As in any Hispano-Islamic garden, water is its lifeblood, found here in a huge variety of forms, trickling down the sides of a small octagonal tank and gathering in a channel before running down a flight of steps.

Left Water flowing from the cistern is collected in this fountain.

Above right A bench, irises and balls of box make this a beguiling corner of the garden.

Below right One of the garden's green rooms, also with rounded forms of box.

The Romeral de San Marcos is a masterpiece which brings together its creator's extraordinary gifts: his artistic soul, his deep learning and his sound technical knowledge. Silva, who was also a painter and engraver, was born in Uruguay. After studying fine art and architecture, he moved to Brazil in the early 1950s and worked with the ground-breaking garden designer Roberto Burle Marx. After spending some years in France, where he studied landscaping at Versailles, he arrived in Spain in 1969, to combine his design work with a career as a teacher. His many public and private gardens draw from the Hispano-Islamic tradition, while always being full of individual touches like his magical flights of steps.

The Romeral was Silva's refuge and his laboratory, a place where, he said, 'I test the virtues and the limitations of the climate, the difficulties in growing some species, and the ease of adapting others.' Against all expectation, he was able to create this garden in the middle of the dry Castilian plain. A symphony of colour, with light and shade in constant evolution according to the hour and the season, it is always the same but always changing.

The friendly maestro left us in 2000, but his spirit lives on in this open-air classroom.

The imposing silhouette of the Alcázar de Segovia appears beyond the cypresses (*Cupressus sempervirens*) and 'Clair Matin' roses.

EL BOSQUE
Béjar, Castilla y León

'I come to my villa not to cultivate crops, but to cultivate my soul,' wrote Cosimo de' Medici in 1462 of his country estate outside Florence.

El Bosque (The Wood), created in 1567 by the 2nd Duke of Béjar, Francisco de Zúñiga y Sotomayor, is a Spanish descendant of the Medici estate: a Renaissance villa designed for contemplation and the pleasures of country life. Even today, in this exceptional ensemble – including *palacete*, gardens, orchards, meadows and wood – the spirit of Italian humanism endures, bearing the influence of the Roman villas described in the letters of Cicero and Pliny the Younger. Following the architect Alberti's recommendations in his classic treatise *De re aedificatoria* (*On the Art of Building*) the villa is positioned on a hillside near the city – only a kilometre from the centre of Béjar – and there is a close relationship between the house and the garden, which is laid out in terraces with decorative and architectural elements including steps, fountains, benches, exedras and small squares. These vestiges of the original garden are now covered in moss and overarched by mature planes and chestnut trees.

If the classical layout evokes Renaissance Italy, the enormous pool in front of the house – the garden's most notable feature – has more exotic associations. With a small island at its centre, now occupied by a nineteenth-century arbour, it resembles those in the great Mughal gardens of northern India and Pakistan, such as the Lake Palace at Udaipur, with its floating pavilion amid great expanses of water. This oriental influence was probably transmitted through Spain's neighbour, Portugal, the first modern European country to make contact with India after the arrival of Vasco da Gama in 1498. There are similar pools with pavilions throughout Portugal – at the beautiful gardens of Quinta das Torres, for example.

The combination of water features, generous fruit gardens and a leafy wood of oak and chestnut is made possible by the abundant natural springs of the nearby Sierra de Candelaria. A delicate balance is

Opposite A nineteenth-century iron pavilion crowns this islet in the large pool next to the house.

Left A fountain with the founders' shields beyond, among an abundance of decorative elements in stone.

maintained between the natural and cultivated landscape, between the wood and the garden.

On the terrace below the pool, a more romantic style speaks of a different era. In 1869 the last Duke of Béjar sold the property, and the new owners exchanged the original geometric structure for a more fashionable design with winding paths and exotic conifers including sequoias, spruces and Spanish firs as well as a magnificent *Magnolia grandiflora*.

An orchard extends further down the hill, where once strawberries, raspberries, apples and pears were grown, watered by channels from the great pool, which served as a reservoir. Lower still, the water collects in another smaller pool. The practical and the beautiful are thus brought together in a unique design which, despite some modifications, retains its original layout.

El Bosque has been owned by the town of Béjar since 1996. In the middle of El Sistema Central, the central mountain range whose granite and greenery divides the province of Castile in two, this is an oasis of serenity and magnificence, a faint echo of oriental tales.

Above Architectural elements evoke the Renaissance.

Right The huge pool is reminiscent of the great Mughal gardens.

REAL MONASTERIO
de San Lorenzo de El Escorial Madrid

For many people, this colossal granite building, both grandiose and austere, is the essence of Castile. Conceived as a monastery, basilica, seminary, pantheon, palace and library, it is more than anything a direct expression of the complex personality of its founder, Philip II. The king was usually perceived as dour and gloomy, but just as his reserve concealed a great love of nature and gardens, the monolithic monastery contains some unexpectedly lovely gardens, originally planted with a great variety of colourful flowers.

The king, master of the greatest territory in history, an empire – twenty times bigger than Rome's – 'where the sun never sets', laid the monastery's foundation stone in 1563 to commemorate his victory over the French in the battle of St Quentin on 10 August 1557, San Lorenzo's day. The architects were Juan Bautista de Toledo and, after his death in 1584, Juan de Herrera, who gave his name to the *herreriano* style which characterizes the building, a sober idiom without superfluous ornamentation, strictly in accordance with Renaissance classicism.

Right The only green space enclosed by the walls of the monastery building, El Patio de Los Evangelistas has a small stone temple with statues of the four evangelists and their attributes.

Opposite The Monks' Garden with the convalescents' gallery to the rear and, on the lower level, the pond, which provided fish for the monks and water for the orchard.

The Escorial is the fruit of Philip's religious fervour as much as his desire to leave an impressive dynastic monument. There is a pantheon, but also a monastic retreat for the king himself, following the Spanish tradition for such things, as his father Charles V had at the monastery of Yuste, where he retired before his death. Directly inspired by Charles's, Philip's lodgings, as bare as a monk's cell, lie next to the basilica's high altar, from where he could hear mass. But while one side gave on to the church, the others provided views of the gardens, which extended below to the south and east: the Monks' Garden and the Gardens of the King and Queen.

Although the gardens seem rigid and severe today, in Philip's time they were full of a great variety of flowering plants, many from the New World. 'There are so many white, blue, yellow and red flowers and other pleasing combinations, and they are so well laid out, that they look like rich carpets from Turkey, Cairo or Damascus,' wrote Prior José de Sigüenza in his *Foundation of the Escorial Monastery*. These sensual spaces were descended from the Hispano-Islamic garden, which was full of colour and scent, where roses mix with pinks, violets, pansies, tulips and lilies. There were also orange and lemon trees here,

protected in winter with oak leaves and great wooden planks.

The gardens' current neoclassical appearance dates from the eighteenth century. Below these long, narrow, elevated gardens are kitchen gardens, watered from a large pond.

The spirit of the Catholic Counter-Reformation which infuses the monastery is best seen in the Patio of the Evangelists, the main cloister. Both the symbol and the representation of a longed-for paradise, this was designed for the monks' recreation and contemplation. The design is based on the number four, representing the order of the world, the four corners of creation. The cloister is therefore a quadrangle divided into four smaller quadrangles with an octagonal temple in the middle, where sculptures of the four evangelists match four fountains in the form of their attributes – the lion, the bull, the angel and the eagle – which flow into four pools.

The patio was originally bright with flowers, but these were replaced in the eighteenth century with the clipped box hedges seen today. Although not historically accurate, this design reflects and develops the sober lines of the monastery, resulting in a uniquely integrated combination of garden and architecture, a work of serene beauty.

Left The severe aspect of this garden dates from the eighteenth century. It was originally full of colourful flowers.

Following pages The huge monastery building, with the fish pond and snow-covered fruit trees in front.

CASITA DEL PRÍNCIPE
San Lorenzo de El Escorial, Madrid

So near and yet so far: from Philip II's austere monastery the visitor passes to the elegance of the neighbouring *casitas* of the Príncipe and the Infante, the Crown Prince and the Prince. While the Escorial – watching over them gloweringly – was built for the salvation of souls, the *casitas* were to serve as relaxing retreats from life at court. Later in construction than the Escorial, they draw from a shared classical tradition, though this is expressed in a different manner. These two little neoclassical jewels are vestiges of an enlightened, cultured and cosmopolitan period in Spain's history.

La Casita del Príncipe, the Crown Prince's Cottage, also known as the Lower Cottage, was built by Juan de Villanueva from 1772 to 1773 for the Prince of Asturias, later to be crowned Charles IV. Both the prince, who had grown up in Naples, where his father had occupied the throne, and the architect, who had spent five years in Rome, felt a great passion for Italy and the classical world. Their shared enthusiasm found expression not only in the design of the house but also in the garden. Ignoring the new landscape style which was sweeping

Hydrangeas (*H. macrophylla*) flourish in the shade of *Magnolia grandiflora*

Europe, Villanueva sought inspiration in the villas of Rome, both ancient and modern, where the geometrical rigour of clipped hedges prevailed. Following classical precepts, Villanueva saw the garden as an extension of the house, echoing its symmetry.

The *casita* offered an escape from the strict etiquette of life at court, where the Spanish monarch still took meals in public. As historian Charles C. Noel notes, 'Charles IV liked to escape from the strictures of court, to take himself off to one of his elegant and enchanting cottages where he himself cooked lamb chops, tortilla and other delicacies.'

The cottage divides the garden in two: a small area at the front and another to the rear, arranged in three terraces that follow the building's structure. Ramps lead to the upper level, where the large water tank which supplies the garden echoes in its simple design the Renaissance tank designed by Juan de Herrera at the Escorial.

The purity of the original design was distorted in the nineteenth century by the planting of large exotic trees, including wellingtonias, cedars and magnolias, to create a more romantic atmosphere. But every cloud has a silver lining. Even if one were to lament this alteration, the hydrangeas that flourish in the resulting shade seem like a true miracle in the harsh dry Castilian summer.

Left The garden's central axis, with its cypress arch.

Above Large exotic trees planted in the nineteenth century make an incongruous background for the clipped box hedges of the original scheme.

Left The greenhouse.

CASITA DEL INFANTE

San Lorenzo de El Escorial, Madrid

'Architecture is frozen music,' wrote Schopenhauer, and by analogy we might say that gardens are living harmonies. The garden has always been linked to music, either as an inspiration or as the perfect setting for its performance and enjoyment.

The Casita del Infante, also known as the Upper Cottage, was designed from the start as a place for music. It was laid out between 1772 and 1773 for Prince Gabriel, the most brilliant son of Charles III, from plans by the great neoclassical architect Juan de Villanueva (see also the Casita del Príncipe, page 128). Gabriel was a prince of the Enlightenment, enthralled by the classical world and

Above The Casita was home to the young Juan Carlos before he became king in 1975.

Left Surrounded by the forest of La Herrería, the garden's hedges trace patterns in clipped box.

133

by music. His tutor, Antonio Soler, was a monk at the great palace-monastery complex of the Escorial and a significant composer who wrote several sonatas for his illustrious pupil. As elsewhere in the courts of Europe, the prince would arrange chamber concerts here for a select group, at which he himself would often perform on the clavichord.

Both Soler's compositions and Villanueva's plans are informed by a sober classicism, in contrast to the exuberance of the Baroque. The layout of the building (*casita* means cottage), with its central assembly room, was modelled on the Palladian villas of sixteenth-century Italy, and shares their balance and simplicity.

In the garden, the same serene harmony prevails. There are Italianate terraces with clipped hedges and low fountains. José Luis Sancho notes in *Jardines Reales de España* that this horizontal design is disrupted by the tall conifers planted at the end of the nineteenth century, when the garden

belonged to the forest engineering school. Villanueva had designed the parterres so that when the family came to stay at the nearby Escorial, from October to early December each year the princes could stroll in the sun.

Like the small but luxurious constructions popular in France at the same time – the *folies*, *trianons* and *bagatelles* – the Casita was conceived as an integral part of the garden, a charming addition to the landscape for the prince and his circle.

However, this eighteenth-century scene of musical evenings was to come to a sudden and tragic end. In 1788, after the loss in childbirth of his wife and baby son, Prince Gabriel himself died at the age of thirty-six. His father, Charles III, was heartbroken and followed his son to the grave barely a month later. They are all interred in the Royal Pantheon at the Escorial, whose imposing silhouette dominates the view from these gardens, which serve as a beautiful reminder of a resplendent age.

The classic layout of box and laurel hedges.

This image of swans with the Escorial in the background brings to mind the mythological seduction of Leda by Zeus in the shape of a swan.

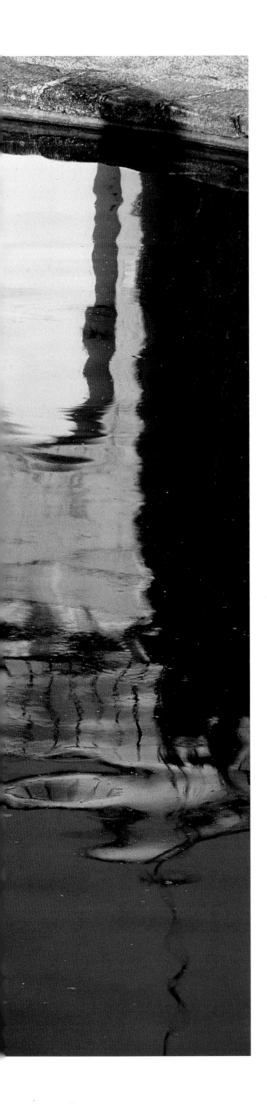

LA QUINTA DEL DUQUE DEL ARCO

Madrid

'Water and fountains are the soul of a garden, and its principal ornament; they animate and awaken the garden, bringing it to life,' wrote Dézallier d'Argenville in his *Theory and Practice of Gardening* in 1709. True to the words of the great French garden writer, water plays the leading role in this baroque garden, from the calm reflective surface of the pool to the fountains' lively jets.

Built on the old royal hunting ground of Monte del Pardo, to the north of Madrid, the Quinta was the country retreat of one of Philip V's great favourites. The Duke of Arco acquired the land in 1717 to create a *palacete* – a small palace – with a garden and orchards, following the custom among aristocrats and courtiers of the time to have a place to relax in on the outskirts of the capital. As with the Italian villas that were their models, these *quintas* were places in which leisure was combined agriculture.

The Duke of Arco, Alonso Manrique de Lara, was one of the great intimates of Spain's first Bourbon monarch. As Master of the King's Horse, he was responsible for all the king's hunting and travel. 'A wild boar charged the king and the duke threw himself in the way and killed it with his sword. He was badly hurt in doing so, and from this action flowed the king's favour and position,' wrote the Duke of Almazán in his *History of Spanish Hunting*. After the Duke of Arco's death, his widow gave the Quinta to Philip V in 1745, ensuring that the name of the loyal courtier would be forever associated with his lord.

The garden's design is attributed to Claude Truchet and dates back to 1726. The garden is laid out in four levels, with terraces adapted to the sloping terrain and an axis of symmetry which curiously does not bear any relation to the house. If the sloping layout brings Italian models to mind, the cascade is like a smaller version of the one at Saint-Cloud near Paris, as the Marquesa de Casa Valdés notes. This mixture of influences and cultures is characteristic of Spanish landscape design even today.

The source of the Quinta's magic is the marvellous interplay of the architectural gardens, the groves of olives and fruit trees and the natural landscape of Monte del Pardo, with its oaks and ilex – the scene of Velazquez' hunting portraits with their unmistakable silver-grey skies.

Left Cypresses and vaulted niches decorate the semicircular wall reflected in the pool.

Above This cascade recalls the one at the Château de Saint-Cloud outside Paris.

Above left Parterres with roses and hedges.

Above right The garden is arranged in terraces around an axis, with the palace to one side. The large conifers (*Sequoiadendron giganteum*), which distort the original design, were planted in the nineteenth century.

JARDINES DEL BUEN RETIRO
Madrid

'El Retiro', they call it in Madrid: the green heart of the capital, its great outdoor room, an area of 118 hectares where musicians, mimes, fortune tellers, caricaturists and peddlers ply their trades. A popular place, full of variety and open to all.

The enlightened Charles III first opened part of the gardens to the public in 1767, on condition that certain dress standards were observed. Entrance was not admitted to anyone unclothed. Gentlemen should have well-combed hair, and no hat, hairnet or cap. Nor, according to the 'Regulations for Pedestrians in the Royal Gardens', could they wear overcoats, raincoat or capes. Although the public had been given access to royal gardens to attend spectacles in the seventeenth century, this regular opening was the first step towards the democratization of Spain's gardens. The first truly public gardens came later, in the nineteenth century, as the Industrial Revolution brought a new density of population to the cities, and a newly pressing need for green space.

The Buen Retiro (Fair Retreat) owes its name to the ancient retreat originally known as the Cuarto Real (Royal Quarters), attached to the monastery of St Jerome, where Spanish monarchs occasionally sought seclusion. This formed the nucleus of the palace complex built during the reign of Philip IV between 1630 and 1640 on what was then the outskirts of Madrid, and covering an area almost half as big as the capital itself. Austere in tone, built in brick with granite mouldings and slate roof tiles, the Salon de los Reinos (Hall of the Kingdoms) and the Casón del Buen Retiro (House of Fair Retreat) are the only remaining parts of the huge original palace of the 'King of the Planet'. Both are now both part of the Prado Museum.

As the historian Consuelo Durán has remarked, the most interesting thing

about the Buen Retiro was always its gardens, though these suffered from the same lack of planning and unity that blighted the original group of buildings: an absence of structure and symmetry which is characteristic of the Spanish concept of space. They were a collection of green spaces, some more formally structured with geometric hedges, others more bosky, with lattice-covered paths, orchards and a series of inhabited hermitages. Water played an important role with pools, channels and fountains. The Great Pond, which can still be seen today, was used for spectacular mock naval battles known as *naumaquias*, as well as providing a setting for works by the great playwrights Calderón de la Barca and Lope de Vega. It is hard to imagine a more atmospheric setting on a summer night with its dense verdure, scents, sounds and cool night air. Courtly entertainments were also staged here – tournaments, bullfights, hunts and banquets.

The garden's golden age came to an end with Philip IV's death in 1665, and the Buen Retiro as it is today owes little to that period. The only remaining traces are the Great Pond and another octagonal pond. Political events and changing fashions in garden design have left their mark over more than three centuries.

The accession of the Bourbon dynasty in the person of Philip V in the early eighteenth century also had an impact on the park. The parterre

Left and above Despite later modifications, the parterre designed by Robert de Cotte in the early eighteenth century retains something of the French Baroque. Box hedges, laurel pyramids, cedars and oddly shaped cypresses occupy this vast space.

141

dates from this period, designed by the French architect Robert de Cotte. Despite nineteenth-century modifications, it is still true to the original layout with its central axis and parterres to either side, a faithful reflection of the French taste for symmetry and open space. This originally formed part of a much larger scheme to convert the sober Habsburg palace into a baroque château.

The Peninsular War of 1808–14 (known in Spain as the War of Independence) was a disaster for the Buen Retiro, as the palace and gardens became the headquarters of the invading French army. Thousands of trees were felled. With the restoration of the Bourbon king, Ferdinand VII, a massive replanting of trees was undertaken and the gardens were opened to the public, with the exception of an area known as the Reserve, where access was restricted to the royal family. A romantic garden was created here, with small picturesque constructions including a fisherman's lodge and an artificial mountain. In the tradition of keeping

Ivy-draped pergolas, low box hedges, clipped cypresses and a central pool are features of the formal gardens designed by head gardener Cecilio Rodríguez in 1941.

exotic animals in royal gardens, the king also created a bestiary, which later became the city's zoo.

In 1868 the gardens passed into public ownership and became the capital's first public park. The carriage drive, which served as a meeting place for the high society of the day, dates from this period, and the beautiful Crystal Palace was built in 1887 to house exotic plants brought over

for the Exhibition of the Philippine Islands. Among many transformations the park has undergone since then, the anachronistic monument from 1922 to Alfonso XII which dominates the Great Pond stands out, as do the spaces created by Cecilio Rodríguez: the 1915 rose garden modelled on the Bagatelle in Paris and the formal gardens of 1941 which bear his name.

Today El Retiro is undoubtedly

Madrid's most emblematic and exciting park. Its evolution continues with the recent creation of the Bosque de los Ausentes (Wood for the Departed) to commemorate the victims of the terrorist attacks of 11 March 2004.

For Madrileños, the Buen Retiro is a breath of fresh green air, a refuge from the harsh Castilian plateau which looms on the horizon.

Left The Crystal Palace was built for the Exhibition of the Philippines in 1887 as a greenhouse for exotic species. Today it holds temporary exhibitions of contemporary art. Swamp cypress (*Taxodium distichum*) grows in the artificial lake.

Above The Octagonal Pool dates from the early days of the garden, when a bridge led to a small pavilion in the centre.

The monument to Alfonso XII, next to the Gran Estanque (great pool) is one of the sights of Madrid. Dating from 1922, this splendid space was designed by the architect José Grasés Riera. With a large colonnade surrounding a bronze statue of the king on horseback by Mariano Benilliure, a flight of stairs decorated with stone lions leading down to the pool, and a host of allegorical sculptures representing aspects of the nation, this theatrical work resembles the monument to Vittorio Emanuele II in Rome.

JARDÍN DE JOAQUÍN SOROLLA

Madrid

To enter this painter's garden is to be immersed in his world: it is a feast for the senses, and its inviting corners promise peace and happiness. Focusing on colour and texture and the play of light and shade, the artist created these scenes to be both lived in and painted. As the artist and garden designer Javier de Winthuysen wrote, 'Sorolla, that lover of colour, has captured in the gardens of his house in Madrid all the brightness and joy of Andalusia and the Mediterranean.'

Joaquín Sorolla, born in Valencia in 1863, is the great Spanish painter of light. Vibrant colours and wide brushstrokes flood his famous beach scenes with the unique light of Spain's Mediterranean coast. He quickly gained worldwide recognition for his work, which also includes folk traditions (such as a major commission from the Hispanic Society of America in New York to record the Spanish regions), landscapes, portraits and garden scenes.

Sorolla was infatuated with Andalusia and returned there again and again to paint. He was fascinated by its architecture and gardens and

The Fuente de las Confidencias (Fountain of Secrets) by the Valencian sculptor Francisco Díaz Pintado presides over this fern-ringed pool where arum lilies grow.

149

intended his house in Madrid to have the same spirit. Construction began in 1910, with a design by the architect Enrique María Repullés, which accommodated the Sorolla household – his wife, Clotilde, and their three children – as well as the artist's studio.

Although Sorolla was involved with the design of the house, his real creation was the garden, a profoundly Andalusian design with a fusion of Hispano-Islamic and Italian elements. The influence of the gardens at Granada's Generalife and Seville's Real Alcázar (see pages 204 and 218) is unmistakable in the tiles, the myrtles, the water channels and the long pool, which combine with echoes of the classical world in the form of statues, vertical columns, laurels and box hedges. The garden was laid

out between 1911 and 1917 in three outdoor rooms, an extension of the house. The sound of the fountains and the scents of jasmine, rose and magnolia evoke the south. Sorolla planted several of the trees himself, including the false acacia (*Robinia pseudoacacia*), the white mulberry (*Morus alba*) and the Judas tree (*Cercis siliquastrum*).

The paintings inside the house – which has been a museum since 1932 – show how Sorolla painted almost every corner of the garden. It was here on 17 June 1920, while working on a portrait of Señora Perez de Ayala, with summer round the corner, the scents of jasmine and magnolia in the air and his brush in his hand, that Sorolla suffered the crippling stroke that led to his death in 1923.

Above and right Two views of a corner of the garden inspired by the Generalife in Granada, with its long pool, low fountain, tiles and criss-crossing jets of water. Myrtle hedges and pots of geraniums complete the scene.

REAL JARDÍN BOTÁNICO
Madrid

A synthesis of art and science, the Jardín Botánico in Madrid is a product of the Enlightenment which pervaded the Bourbon court in the second half of the eighteenth century. Charles III – who well deserves his nickname 'Madrid's greatest mayor' – founded the garden in 1774 as part of a plan to promote science that included the work of the Observatory and the Museum of Natural Sciences (now the Prado Museum).

There was a botanical garden at Soto de Migas Calientes on the outskirts of Madrid as early as 1755, founded by Ferdinand VI for the cultivation of medicinal and exotic plants. In the same year a multidisciplinary expedition including the Swedish botanist Peter Löfling, star pupil of the father of modern botany Carl Linnaeus, set off to explore the

river Orinoco between Venezuela and Columbia. This was the first of several overseas expeditions that established Spain as a world power in botany. Although Löfling did not survive the journey, his studies of South American and Spanish flora were published posthumously as *Iter Hispanicum* in 1758. This forms part of the Jardín Botánico's archive, which documents the expeditions sponsored by the Spanish Crown and also includes a herbarium and thousands of drawings and botanical prints.

The rose garden, with its wealth of old roses. The beds are edged with box, and there is a neoclassical granite fountain at the centre.

As the inscription above the Puerta del Rey (King's Gate) makes clear, the aim of the garden, which opened to the public in 1781, was to spread knowledge of science and its medicinal, culinary and industrial applications among the people: 'Carolus III P.P. BOTANICES INSTAURATOR CIVIUM SALUTI ET OBLECTAMENTO ANNO MDCCLXXXI' (Charles III, father of the homeland, restorer of the botanical garden for the health and recreation of his subjects, 1781).

Although Linnaeus never visited Madrid, his revolutionary system for the classification of species determines the clarity and simplicity of the garden's current layout. This is the work of Juan de Villanueva, who in 1780 took over from the Italian architect Sabatini the work he had

begun in 1775. Retaining Sabatini's three distinct levels, Villanueva replaced complicated parterres with simpler, plainer designs, well suited to the rational exegesis of scientific learning. Entering through the neoclassical Puerta de Murillo, which is also Villaneuva's work, one can appreciate the austere design of the Terrace of the Squares, with its collection of edible, aromatic and ornamental plants, arranged in squares with a granite fountain at the centre of each. Within each square, borders in simple geometrical forms are edged with low box hedges.

The second level – known as the Terrace of the Botanical Schools, in reference to the Linnaean system – follows the same pattern, with a collection of plants arranged according to their botanical affinity.

The upper terrace has a quite different character. Remodelled in the mid-nineteenth century, this has a romantic style with winding paths and high hedges of viburnum. The glass and iron greenhouse, which houses tropical plants, aquatic plants and bryophytes, also dates from

Above left Dahlias were first collected on Martín Sessé's botanical expedition to Mexico.

Left Azaleas flourish in the garden.

Right Beneath towering cyresses, a rectangular bed planted with irises.

Following pages Tulips bloom among the sober lines of box on the Terraza de los Cuadros (Terrace of the Squares).

Top Beech (Fagus sylvatica)

Left Agave americana

Above Miscanthus sinensis

Right Acer saccharinum

Far right Physalis alkekengi

this period, as does the elliptical pond with a bust of Linnaeus in the middle. Villanueva's work is still visible in two other pools, a wrought-iron pergola bearing Spanish vines and the magnificent building now known as the Villanueva Pavilion. This was originally conceived as a pair of glasshouses connected by a lecture theatre, where the great botanist Antonio José Cavanilles delivered lectures.

At its height the Botanical Garden was an international centre of excellence, but Spain's profound state of crisis during the nineteenth century took its toll on the garden, which shrank in size and even came to accommodate a zoo. The following century began just as badly, and the garden entered a long period of neglect, until its splendid restoration between 1974 and 1981 at the hands of the garden designer Leandro Silva. The most recent additions have been a new glasshouse in 1993 and the creation of a fourth terrace in 2005, higher and smaller than the others, holding a collection of bonsai trees.

Today, with its 5,000 species spread over 8 hectares, the Jardín Botánico is a sanctuary of beauty and learning, a living encyclopaedia where plant names can be learnt at the calm pace of a pleasant stroll. As Linnaeus put it, 'If you don't know the names of things, what you know of them disappears.'

EL CAPRICHO
Madrid

Above The lake and the island, with a cascade next to a monument to the 3rd Duke of Osuna. To the right is the Casa de Cañas (Cane House), covered in bamboo.

Opposite The Temple of Bacchus with a Judas tree (*Cercis siliquastrum*) in flower.

El Capricho (The Caprice) is as original, fantastical and extravagant as its name suggests. Entering this garden in the suburbs of Madrid, you forget the humdrum surroundings and lose yourself in an imaginary landscape, an Arcadia strewn with follies including a miniature castle and a giant apiary. This magical kingdom was the perfect setting for the grand outdoor receptions of former times.

The garden was created in the 1780s by one of Spain's leading noblewomen, Maria Josefa Alonso Pimentel, Duchess of Osuna, 'the most outstanding lady in Madrid for her merits, talents and taste', according to her contemporary Lady Holland. With her husband, the 9th Duke of Osuna, the duchess was patron to intellectuals, musicians and artists, who often gathered at El Capricho. Goya was her favourite, and their close relationship resulted in magnificent works such as the portrait of the duchess with her husband and their four children which now hangs in the Prado Museum in Madrid.

Cultured and cosmopolitan, the duchess was aware of the new garden styles in France and England, which at that time had barely made an impact in Spain. In pursuit of the Rousseau-esque ideal of 'a return to nature', she created what is now regarded as the most important landscape garden in Spain.

The palace – built between 1792 and 1795 by Mateo Guill and Manuel

Machuca – and its 14 hectares of gardens were at the centre of an estate the duke and duchess acquired in 1783. A formal axis runs from the entrance and includes an exedra in the Plaza of the Roman Emperors, later adorned with a bust in the duchess's honour by her grandson. In the lower gardens, a laurel maze was replanted in 1987, following the original design.

But the great innovation was the landscape garden on the upper level, where paths meander across a gently undulating meadow, and a stream leads to a lake.

The garden was initially the work of Pablo Boutelou, the royal gardener, whose design was only partly carried out. According to Victoria Soto Caba, it was the French gardeners Jean Baptiste Mulot and later Pierre Provost who shaped the garden we see today.

161

The real highlights are the decorative buildings, which create unexpected panoramas throughout the romantic landscape. Among these follies is the Casa de la Vieja, or Old Woman's House, which imitates and idealizes a country labourer's cottage. Instead of a real peasant family like that installed by Marie Antoinette in her Hameau at Versailles, this cottage was peopled with clockwork models, made by the Milanese stage designer Maria Tadey, who worked for the duchess between 1792 and 1795. Maria Tadey was also responsible for the Hermitage and the Chinese-style boathouse on the lake, called the Cane House after its bamboo exterior. The Hermitage, decorated with *trompe-l'oeil* designs both inside and out, was home to Brother Arsenio (buried next to the temple) and later Brother Eusebio, genuine hermits who formed part of El Capricho's sentimental landscape. The hermits were later replaced by a dummy.

The most curious building of all, and the one that best exemplifies El Capricho's Enlightenment spirit, is the Apiary, a neoclassical pavilion

Above This miniature fortress is surrounded by a moat. It originally had a drawbridge, twelve cannons and a clockwork soldier.

where beehives are set into one wall, with their openings looking outwards. Windows inside the building allow visitors to watch the bees in their hives.

Next door is the Temple of Bacchus, originally dedicated to Venus, and surrounded by Judas trees (*Cercis siliquastrum*).

In 1815 the duchess commissioned Antonio Lopez Aguado to make a neoclassical dance pavilion above the spring which fed the artificial stream, allowing guests to arrive here by boat.

The garden remained in the Osuna family until 1882 when, on the death of the 12th duke, who during a life of extravagance had dissipated one of the greatest fortunes in Spain, it was sold off at auction. It changed hands again a number of times before the Civil War of 1936–9, when it served as the headquarters for the defence of Madrid. The legacy of this time is still visible in a number of bunkers next to the palace.

Since 1974 the garden has been the property of the city of Madrid, and has been much restored. Today this enchanting place conveys the magic of a forgotten world.

Above A neoclassical exedra, remodelled in the nineteenth century.

Following pages The oval Temple of Bacchus, originally dedicated to Venus, with the palace beyond.

REAL SITIO DE ARANJUEZ
Aranjuez, Madrid

To the south of Madrid, by the river Tajo, lies Aranjuez, a genuine oasis in the inhospitable Castilian plain. It is what the ancient Persians called a *pairidaeza* (from which our word 'paradise' derives), an enclosed garden: the concept of paradise as a place apart, to which only the privileged few have access. The scene of sumptuous feasts, it was once a magical world full of exotic plants and animals where the Spanish court spent carefree and playful months every spring. The gardens of Aranjuez have also inspired artists, poets and musicians. Joaquín Rodrigo captured their essence in his famous Concierto de Aranjuez, claiming that 'the scent of the magnolias, the song of the birds and the fountains' sigh live forever in the melody.'

Today the Real Sitio de Aranjuez is an extraordinary mix of different eras, a combination of architecture and town planning, and with gardens both ornamental and productive, the source of delicious strawberries and asparagus.

Aranjuez dates back to the fifteenth century, when the original medieval palace passed from the knights of the Order of St James of Compostela to the 'Catholic monarchs' Ferdinand and Isabella. Their grandson, Philip II, began work on a new Renaissance-style palace in 1561, employing the architects he had used for the Escorial (see page 122), Juan Bautista de Toledo and Juan de Herrera (although the building was not completed until the second half of the eighteenth century). The king, a garden enthusiast,

Above and right Geometrical box hedges in the Island Garden.

Below The Fuente de Arpías (Fountain of Harpies) with *El Niño de la Espina* (*The Boy with the Thorn*). The central piece was cast from the Hellenistic original.

gave instructions for the King's Garden to be created next to the palace: this intimate, secluded space surrounded by high walls was a secret garden in the Italian style.

The Island Garden, on a triangle formed by the junction of a canal and the river Tajo, also dates from Philip's reign. The Renaissance layout shows the influence of the Flemish designers who worked here alongside Frenchmen and Germans.

This is a sober place, with narrow paths that were originally covered to form tunnels, and a central axis that brings together a series of small *plazas*, which were enclosed by wooden lattices and decorated with fountains. The space around is divided into little compartments delineated by box hedges; in Philip's day these compartments contained knots of aromatic plants including mugwort, rosemary and santolina, filled in with flowers either planted in masses or randomly sown.

Demonstrating a Renaissance taste for the exotic, the Island Garden held an enormous range of plants, from as far away as Asia and the Americas, and animals from far-flung places, including ostriches and camels, which were used to work the garden.

Above right The Fuente de Apolo (Fountain of Apollo), surrounded by tiles and chestnut trees, on the Island Garden.

Below right El Jardín del Rey (King's Garden) next to the palace.

Reshaped in the seventeenth and eighteenth centuries, the garden enjoyed a splendid period in the reign of Philip IV, who used it as a great outdoor room. Thus it became the scene of great feasts and spectacles. The Marquesa de Casa Valdés relates how in 1622 the garden was converted into a torchlit theatre for the king's birthday. The queen and her ladies put on a performance of *La Gloria de Niquea*, written by the Count of Villamediana, who according to popular legend was hopelessly in love with the queen. Shortly after the play began, the scenery caught fire and the king, going to rescue his wife, found her in the arms of Villamediana. It is said that the count started the fire in order to get his hands on the queen. Whether this is true or not, Villamediana was to live for only another four months.

While the Island Garden retains the Renaissance mood of the Habsburg period, the Prince's Garden is one of the earliest examples of the landscape garden in Spain. It was created by Charles IV between 1772, when he was the Prince of Asturias, and 1804. The principal designers were Juan de Villanueva and Pablo Boutelou, scion of a distinguished French family of gardeners.

The ancient orchard in the Jardín del Príncipe (Prince's Garden) with Rusiñol's pavilion in the middle.

The rolling parkland is in reality composed of a series of gardens, which overlie the old orchards and mix formal and more natural styles: an enchanted wood full of surprise and stimulation. Fountains dedicated to Narcissus, Apollo, Neptune and countless others transport visitors to the world of myth, only to astonish them with picturesque scenes including a Chinese pond with a Greek temple, an oriental pavilion, a grotto and an obelisk. This dream world is filled with massive trees, many of them from far away; these include the results of scientific expeditions, for instance these trees from the southern United States – swamp cypress (*Taxodium distichum*), tulip trees (*Liriodendron tulipifera*) and American persimmon (*Diospyros virginiana*).

The ever-present river Tajo provides an unexpectedly maritime atmosphere. It was the means by which a fleet of imitation galleys and gondolas would transport the court, accompanied by music and spectacle, to new adventures in this Castilian Arcadia.

Left La Fuente de Narciso (Fountain of Narcissus), enclosed by planes and chestnut trees, in the Jardín del Príncipe.

Right A view along one of the alleys in the Jardín del Príncipe.

Following pages The Chinese pond in the Jardín del Príncipe, with a Greek temple and a Chinese pavilion.

JARDÍN DE LA REAL FÁBRICA DE PAÑOS

Brihuega, Castilla la Mancha

'The garden of the factory is a romantic garden, a garden to die in when one is very young, of love, or desperation, of consumption and nostalgia,' wrote Camilo José Cela in his *Journey to the Alcarria* (as translated by Frances M. Lopex-Morillas). This is the garden as an emotional refuge, infused with nostalgia and brimming with symbols. Like a garden in some medieval romance, it feels like an idealized setting for flirtatious games. The slight air of decay only serves to strengthen the romantic character of the place, creating a lyrical realm for dreams and their realization.

Dating from the mid-nineteenth century, the garden is on a high terrace overlooking the town of Brihuega and the valley of the river Tajuña. It is anchored by the extraordinary Royal Cloth Mill, a unique industrial building. Dedicated to the production of cloth for military uniforms, this was

Left These resilient Chusan palms (*Trachycarpus fortunei*) exemplify the nineteenth-century taste for exotic species.

Above With a formal design of annuals, box hedges, cypress arches and an old wooden birdhouse, the garden is ineffably romantic.

established in 1750 and formed part of a network of factories created along Enlightenment principles in an attempt to develop Spanish industry. Active until the start of the Civil War in 1936, the factory passed into private hands in 1840, when local businessman Justo Hernández Pareja began to create, in a narrow area where fabric from the factory used to be dried, the romantic garden that survives today.

An archetypal nineteenth-century garden, it has beds hedged with box (*Buxus sempervirens*) and *Lonicera nitida* and bowers that are occupied by evocative features such as an old aviary, now empty, a pavilion, almost overwhelmed by creepers, and a rough stone table. Tall cypresses form arches and a gallery by the balustrade, and bring to mind the traditional Hispano-Islamic garden, where intimate spaces give on to wider perspectives, creating a dialogue between the garden and the surrounding landscape.

The Chusan palms (*Trachycarpus fortunei*), which are also typical of the period, survive the rigours of this region's continental climate, which is felt here with force. Winters are icy, spring is an explosion of colour and the summer sun is scorching, while autumn unfolds with a languid orange beauty.

The circular factory building, with large windows for natural light and ventilation. To the right is a pavilion covered in creepers.

This nineteenth-century garden
was developed on a terrace
overlooking the town of Brihuega.

MONASTERIO DE PIEDRA
Nuévalos, Aragón

Few places blend art and nature as thoroughly as this romantic garden, designed for the contemplation of the dramatic cascades, caves and natural lakes of its majestic landscape. In spite of its natural appearance, the garden, like any other, is artificial – that is to say, man-made – and uses nature as a raw material. But the art of gardening is to reproduce not simply the outward forms of nature – what philosophers called *natura naturata* – but also its inner workings, *natura naturans*.

Dating from 1860, this garden follows the landscape tradition in attempting to blur the boundary between it and its surroundings by adapting itself to them. The English *Fraser's Magazine* wrote at the time: 'In regard to its scenery, the proprietor found that nature had left him little to do but to wonder and adore. Happily he had the good sense to be contented with this; merely bringing into view and making accessible curiosities and points of interest without attempting to improve what in its wild simplicity and grandeur is already perfect.' The proprietor in question was Juan Federico Muntadas, whose superb marriage of garden and

Far left above Cascada La Caprichosa

Far left below Cascada de los Fresnos

Left The waters of the river Piedra are omnipresent, forming spectacular cascades and natural lakes, and turning the place into a paradise in the middle of what is almost a desert zone.

natural landscape is imbued with his taste for the romantic and picturesque, like a scene from a painting by Caspar David Friedrich, where man stands diminished by nature's grandeur.

Muntadas's interventions were as much to make this extraordinary landscape accessible – opening up roads and passes, building bridges and flights of steps – as to lay out a landscape garden, with inviting paths between ash, walnut and plane trees. His father, Pablo Muntadas, acquired the twelfth-century Cistercian monastery at auction in 1840 in a sale of church lands instigated by Mendizábal. Pablo's plan had been to develop the estate as farmland, but his son Juan Federico's discovery of the astonishing Gruta Iris, or Iris Cave, led him to open the park to the public, and by the 1860s it was a tourist attraction. The enterprising Juan Federico, a writer and member of the Spanish Parliament, also founded the first fish farm in Spain, a neat combination of the useful and the beautiful.

The magnificent grounds of the Monasterio de Piedra are quite simply an extraordinary union of man and his environment, a paradigm of the romantic sensibility. Hidden among the folds of the Iberian massif, its location in one of Aragon's driest regions makes it all the more precious; watered by the river Piedra from which the monastery takes its name, this mass of greenery appears like a vision.

Left and right The landscape garden in the valley harmonizes perfectly with the natural surroundings, including this avenue of plane trees.

EL PATIO DE LOS NARANJOS Córdoba

El Patio de los Naranjos is regarded as Europe's oldest living garden. It dates back to the eighth century and the construction of the Mosque of Córdoba, which along with the Alhambra is the most important built achievement of Hispano-Islamic culture.

It is a magnificent example of how to combine gardening and architecture, a place where the rows of trees outside are the continuation of the forest of columns inside. Such refinement reflects the sophistication of the culture of Al-Andalus and the

Caliphate of Córdoba, which with a million inhabitants was at the turn of the first millennium the largest city in the world, and a highly important cultural, political and economic centre. Holding up to twenty thousand people, the mosque was the site

Above Oranges, palms and cypresses grow today where once worshippers made their ablutions.

of religious, social and political gatherings.

Both patio and mosque were built in the 780s on the site of a Visigoth basilica, and expanded successively until 988. After the Christian conquest of Córdoba in 1236 the mosque was converted, with some modifications, into a Catholic sanctuary. Like a Russian doll, this immense building holds a surprise inside: a solemn cathedral begun in the sixteenth century in the reign of Charles V.

Until the Christian period the mosque opened on to the patio, allowing the total fusion of interior and exterior, and forming a continuous space where columns give way to tree trunks, originally of palm, cypress and olive (the last of these providing

Top The pato is divided into sections, each with a fountain.

Above Roman columns were reused in the mosque.

oil for the lamps in the mosque). The orange trees which give the patio its name came in the tenth century, when – along with many other species including lemons, apricots, bananas, rice, cotton, sugar cane, dates and aubergines – they were introduced by the Arabs to Spain.

These bitter oranges (*Citrus aurantium*), originating in South-east Asia, were used for perfume, preserves and medicines. Because of their attractive appearance, orange trees became central to Hispano-Islamic gardening and were planted in streets, gardens and patios.

Today there are ninety-eight splendid orange trees, planted in rows to create a dense green shade all year round, with the beauty of cheerful fruits in winter and aromatic blossom to perfume the spring air. The trees are watered by a network of channels, which cover the patio and provide another interesting example of the combination of the useful and the beautiful that is characteristic of the Hispano-Islamic garden: evaporating water also cools the air – a useful feature indeed in a place where summer temperatures can exceed 40°C.

During the Muslim period, the patio served as a place for people to make their ablutions before entering the mosque to pray; but it was also a place to relax and socialize. It could be seen as the city's most important park, open to everyone, serving as a reminder of the delights awaiting the faithful after death, as a verse from the Koran inscribed on the mosque's interior makes explicit: 'Do not be afraid and do not be sad! Rejoice in the greater garden you have been promised.' Here once again is the timeless idea of the garden as a foretaste of paradise, an idyllic place brimming with peace.

Right A sophisticated system of irrigation channels runs over the patio. Their Spanish name, *acequia*, derives from the Arabic *sakiya*.

Above A rectangular baroque fountain from the seventeenth century.

PALACIO DE VIANA
Córdoba

There is nowhere better than this beguiling maze of intimate, enclosed gardens to grasp the essential nature of the patio, the millennia-old Mediterranean paradigm which allows contemplation of the infinite from indoors. As Borges put it in *Buenos Aires Fervour:* 'Heaven pours into the house down the patio's slope.'

The Palacio de Viana, renowned for its garden and twelve patios, dates from the fourteenth century but takes its name from the 2nd Marquis of Viana, José Saavedra y Salamanca, who completely restored it at the turn of the twentieth century. It remained in the family (who also owned the magnificent garden of Moratalla in the Córdoban Sierra) until 1980, when it was sold to Caja Sur, a bank, and turned into a museum.

Touring the palace is a thrilling journey through different styles of patio, starting with the Patio de Recibo or Welcoming Patio, whose glorious paving is surrounded by a colonnade which has its origins in the Roman peristyle. Patios – the word may come from the Latin *patere*, 'to lie open' – derive ultimately from Mesopotamia but came to Spain with the Romans. Roman houses were organized around an atrium, an open space that was the centre of the home, as can be seen in the remains of Pompeii and Herculaneum. The Moorish occupation of Iberia added the concept of the garden as an oasis to this inheritance, resulting in the creation of retreats rich in scent and colour, and designed for contemplation and the delight of the senses. The patios at Viana abound with aromatic plants, including *Cestrum nocturnum*, *Viola odorata* and *Jasminum officinale*. Bougainvillea, banksia and plumbago add colour to the walls, and hedges of box, myrtle and cypress form a green framework.

Water is a fundamental element of any patio and here it is drawn from the old Roman well which supplies fountains and jets and irrigates the patios and the garden. Pots are also essential, and here they are found everywhere, from the noble Patio del Archivo (Patio of the Archive) and Patio de La Madama (Patio of the Lady) to the humble Patio de los Gatos (Cat Patio), which reproduces a neighbourhood patio with its laundry basin and pots of geraniums clinging to the walls to form a vertical garden.

Within its enclosing walls, the garden seems somehow like the older brother

Left Orange trees a hundred years old flank the pool in the Patio de los Naranjos (Patio of the Orange Trees) at the Palacio de Viana. Beds of *Agapanthus africanus* are ringed by box hedges.

Right A view of the garden from the Patio de la Alberca (Patio of the Pool).

of the patios. Classical in its design, with geometrical hedges, a central fountain and a covered arbour, the space is perfectly in harmony with the architecture of the palace. A centuries-old *Quercus rotundifolia* dominates the space, while slender date palms and mandarin, lemon and orange trees offer a dense green canopy which provides the shade so necessary in this hot land.

Patios are the soul of Córdoba's homes, and thanks to its climate they can be enjoyed almost all year round. The city celebrates its patios in a popular festival, the Concurso de Patios, which throws them open to the public every May. But sadly the patio is threatened by the pressures of speculative development. Instead of offering these marvellous interior landscapes, new buildings tend to be hermetically sealed, with no trace of plants, the cheerful pots replaced by large air conditioning units which disfigure the walls.

One visit to the symphony of outdoor rooms at Viana, with its abundance of scents, sounds, light and shade, is all it takes to understand the patio's benefits to body and soul.

Above left Pots of *Cineraria maritima* on pedestals surround the fountain in the Patio de las Rejas (Patio of the Grille). Citrus trees climb the walls on trellises.

Below left This fountain decorated with pots of pelargoniums is in the centre of the garden, surrounded by box hedges laid out in the shape of a cross.

Above In the Patio de los Naranjos, a fountain with pots of *Bergenia cordifolia* and walls covered with bougainvillea and wisteria.

Right A water jet in the Patio de la Capilla (Patio of the Chapel).

LA ALHAMBRA
Granada

The Alhambra is one of the world's legendary gardens, the incarnation of an exotic, enchanting scene from the tales of the *Arabian Nights*. 'The transition was almost magical; it seemed as if we were at once transported into othertimes [*sic*] and another realm, were treading the scenes of Arabian history,' Washington Irving wrote of his first visit in *Tales of the Alhambra*, whose publication in 1829 led to this becoming an obligatory stop on the Grand Tours of the nineteenth century. Today three million visitors a year are still captivated by its unique magic, deriving from a perfect combination of garden, architecture and landscape.

The location is spectacular. Protected by the high peaks of the Sierra Nevada, and bordered by the river Darro, the Alhambra perches on a steep hill dominating the city of Granada and its fertile plain. In 1239 the founder of the Nasrid dynasty began work on the site of the ancient fortification there, perhaps dating from Roman times, and created a complex of palaces fit for the reign of the last Islamic kingdom of Iberia. His creation reached its apogee in the fourteenth century with the construction of the famous Patio de los Leones (Court of the Lions) and the Patio de Comares (Court of Comares), also known as

the Patio de Arrayanes (Court of Arrayanes). The leitmotif here, as throughout the palace, is water in its various forms: the symbol of life and prosperity which unites exterior and interior, the useful and the beautiful.

The Patio de Comares is part of the Alhambra's public area, and the tower of the same name houses the sultan's throne room. Today's visitor still experiences something of the awe that emissaries waiting to enter the royal presence must have felt when they stood before the vast watery mirror reflecting the surrounding architecture and the sky above. The design is simplicity itself: a rectangular pool with a low fountain at either end, myrtle hedges down the sides and an elegant white marble pavement. Although the original planting was probably more exuberant, in its current form this is a superb example of containment and austerity, a total fusion of architecture and garden.

The Patio de los Leones belongs to a more intimate area of the palace complex, at the heart of the ruling family's private apartments. It takes its name from the iconic fountain at its centre, supported by figures of twelve lions and fed by four channels flowing from the private rooms.

This cruciform design derives from the traditional Persian *chahar bagh*

The Palacio de Partal with its great central pool dates from the fourteenth century and is the oldest building in the complex. However, the gardens here were made in the twentieth century.

or 'quartered garden', which Muslims adopted as a metaphor for the Koran's description of paradise as having four rivers, of honey, milk, water and wine respectively. (The same image is found in the book of Genesis, in which four rivers flow from Eden.) The 124 narrow alabaster columns supporting the gallery that surrounds this patio evoke an oasis of palm trees, completing the exquisite image of heaven on earth.

It is conjectured that the four parterres may originally have been sunken, or planted with randomly strewn flowers to create an effect similar to that of Persian rugs.

While the cruciform garden, which became the prototype for gardens throughout the Islamic world, is Persian in origin, the architectural basis of the patio garden, with its paving and colonnades, is Roman, and was

well rooted in Spain centuries before the Moorish conquest.

The human scale of these spaces is light years away from the Western idea of a royal palace such as Versailles in France, which is designed to contain and intimidate a multitude. To gain a sense of its delicate intimacy, it is best to enjoy the Alhambra quietly – no easy undertaking today amid the avalanche of visitors.

Left The elegant reflecting pool at the centre of the Patio de Comares fuses garden with architecture, earth with sky.

Above Tiles in the Patio del Cuarto Dorado (Patio of the Golden Room).

Right This window in the Salón de los Embajadores (Salon of the Ambassadors), also known as the Salón del Trono (Salon of the Throne), was originally filled with stained glass.

Following pages The Patio de los Leones, with its central fountain and water channels connecting interior and exterior, was the focus of family life for the Nasrid dynasty.

After Granada fell in 1492 to the Christian forces of Ferdinand and Isabella, thus completing the religious, political and cultural unification of Spain, the Alhambra became a royal palace for the Catholic monarchs. Unusually for the era, the conquerors appreciated their prize and hardly altered the structure. They began a programme to restore the fragile Nasrid architecture and converted some rooms into royal apartments. In 1527 their grandson, the Holy Roman Emperor Charles V, added an impressive Renaissance palace to the complex, and the Patio de la Lindaraja (Court of Lindaraja) next to the emperor's private rooms also dates from this time.

With the accession of the Bourbon dynasty to the throne in the early eighteenth century decline set in, and the ancient palaces, in ever worsening condition, were occupied by vagrants. The final indignity came when the palace was used as a barracks by Napoleon's troops during the Peninsular War, and the subsequent demolition of eight of the ancient towers in 1812.

The Alhambra had been a source of fascination to travellers for centuries, but it was the romantic writers and artists of nineteenth-century France,

Britain and America, astonished by its unique oriental appeal, who broadcast its fame across Europe. Extensive restoration was carried out during the twentieth century, and the Partal Palace gardens were created in the 1920s.

Despite their reputation as the best-preserved medieval gardens in Europe, the gardens at the Alhambra, being – like all gardens – made of ephemeral materials, have been subject to countless modifications over the years. But amid so much beauty, considerations of authentic and false, ancient and modern, myth and reality are best set aside. Better to succumb to the charms of the place, taking heed of the popular saying 'There is no fate worse than to be blind in Granada.'

Left The Patio de la Lindaraja, created in the sixteenth century next to the private rooms of Emperor Charles V.

Above A view of Granada from the Alhambra.

Right A dwarf pomegranate (*Punica granatum* var. *nana*) in autumn.

EL GENERALIFE
Granada

An uphill stroll from the Alhambra leads to another of the world's great gardens: the Generalife, whose Arabic name translates as 'highest and most noble of gardens'. This hilltop villa was built as a summer retreat for the ruling Nasrid dynasty in the early fourteenth century, so they could immerse themselves in nature and country life. It was amply surrounded by terraced gardens and orchards – outdoor rooms which created a sense of

intimacy and enclosure – while at the same time offering superb views over one of the most beautiful landscapes in the world: the Alhambra, Granada and the lowlands beyond.

The view is only one of the ingredients in this garden, which is a true feast for the senses with its heady scents, exquisite fruits and the hypnotic murmur of the waters that are the garden's soul. With their desert origins, the Moors valued this liquid

element the most highly of all Spain's delights; they developed the hydraulic traditions left by the Romans, and augmented them with new irrigation techniques from Persia, Egypt and Syria. The marvellous gardens of the Alhambra and the Generalife would be inconceivable without the Acequia Real (Royal Canal), built by the founder of the Nasrid dynasty in the thirteenth century: this carries the waters of the river Darro to deep reservoirs and then on through an aqueduct to the gardens.

The first stop on this tour is the Patio de la Acequia (Patio of the Water Channel), where the omnipresence of water in many forms makes this for many people to be the purest expression of the Hispano-Islamic garden. In fact, nothing could be further from the truth. The famous spouting fountains that cross the central channel were added by the garden's Italian owners in the nineteenth century and have more in common with romantic tastes than the Islamic ideal of still waters reflecting the heavens above. Excavations carried out in 1958 revealed that the garden had originally been cruciform in design, with a central font and four octagonal sunken beds. In the traditional manner, the garden was

Left The Patio de la Acequia with its famous water jets, which in fact were added in the nineteenth century.

Above and following pages A fountain in the Jardines Nuevos (New Gardens) of 1951, designed by the architect Francisco Prieto Moreno, between the Alhambra and the Generalife.

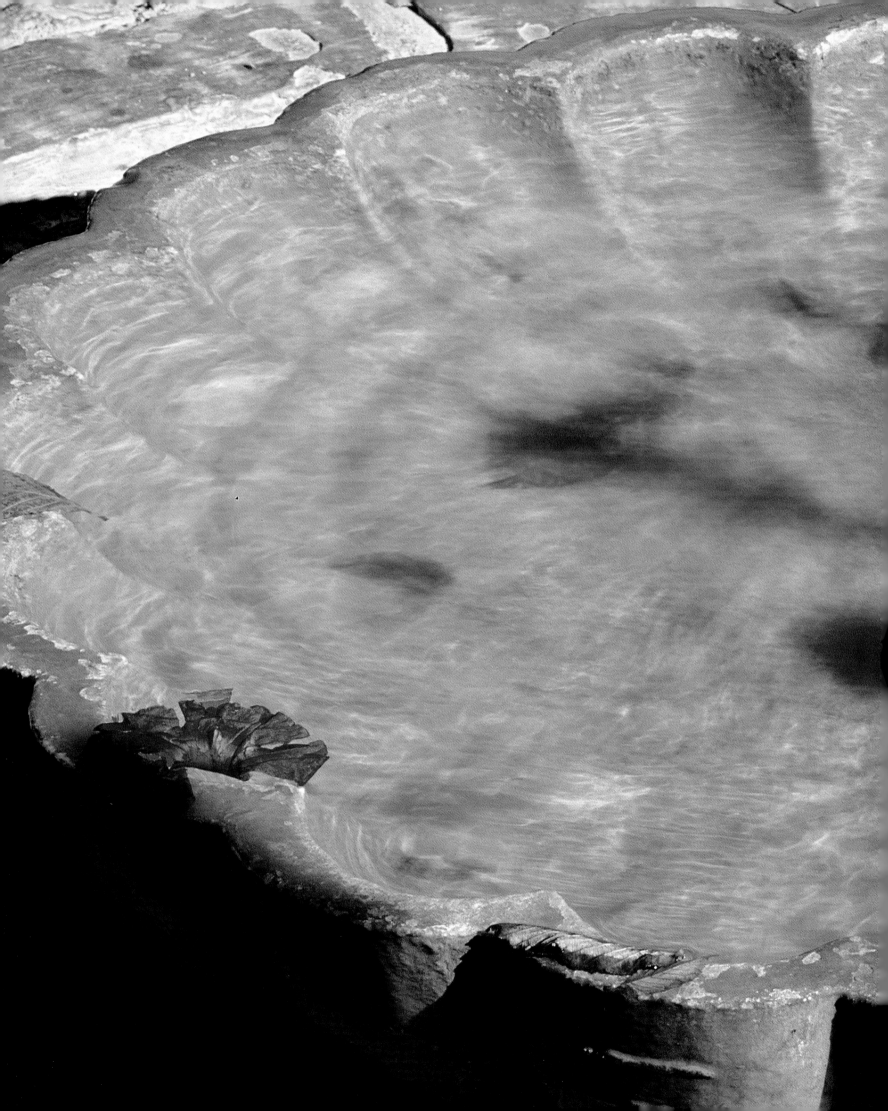

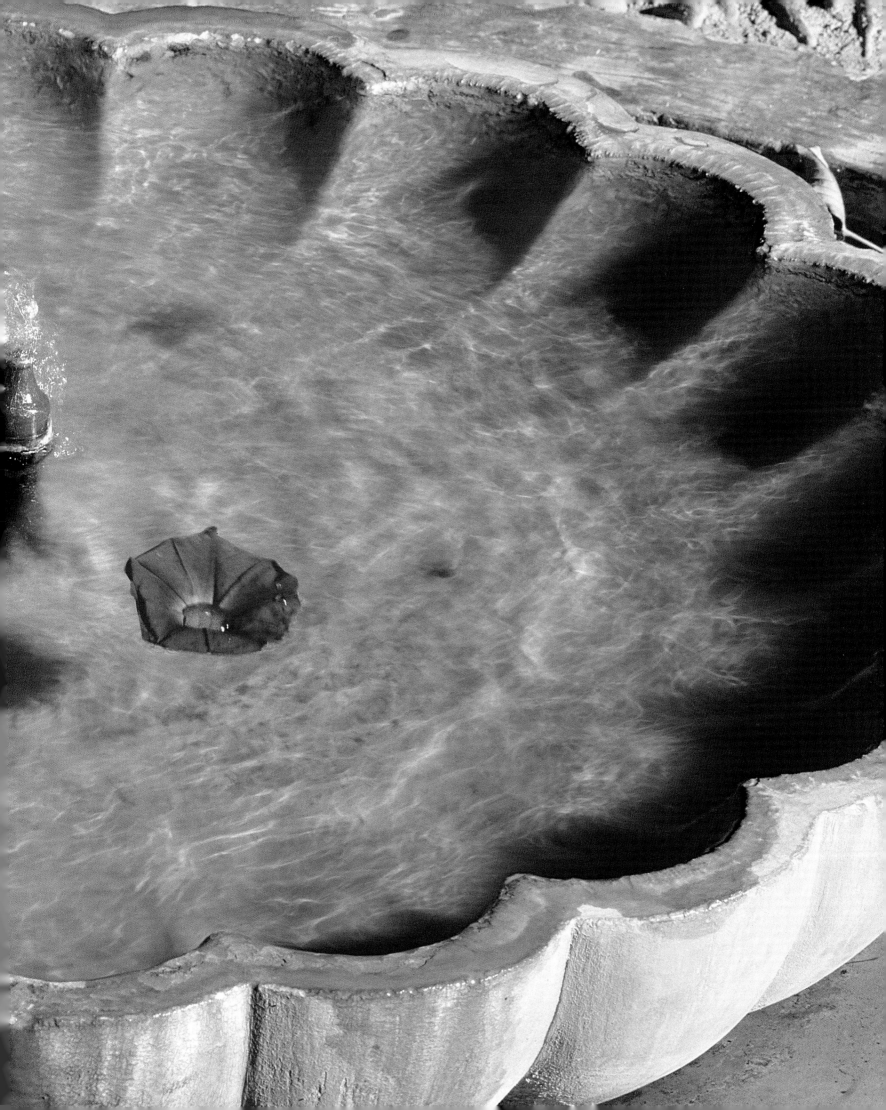

closed off from the outside world. Only low windows in the middle of the western wall allowed views of the surrounding landscape for those seated on the ground. The open lateral corridor and the second storey of the building at the end of the garden, which have transformed the original look of the patio, are later additions from the Christian period.

The tour continues with the Patio del Ciprés de la Sultana (Patio of the Sultana's Cypress), which has a very different atmosphere. Italian style dominates here, with a double-arched gallery and a U-shaped pool with a Renaissance-style basin in the middle, surrounded by high jets of water. The palace's baths were here in the Moorish period. The patio takes its name from the trunk of a withered

cypress (*Cupressus sempervirens*), said to have shaded secret assignations between the wife of the last Moorish king, Boabdil, and a noble of the Abencerrajes family. When they were discovered, the cuckolded king had the whole family beheaded, and their blood is still said to stain the fountain in the Alhambra's Sala de Abencerrajes. It is impossible to forget that both the Generalife and the

Alhambra are settings for an endless series of myths and legends, which has turned them into dreamlike places where magic and reality have been stirred together.

The real jewel of the Nasrid period is the Escalera de Agua (Water Staircase), which linked the Generalife with a small oratory on the hilltop, today replaced by a nineteenth-century viewpoint. Beneath a vault

of laurels, the steps ascend in three flights, broken by landings with low fountains, and flanked by low walls where water from the Acequia Real runs at hand height. This is an enchanting place, fresh and shady: a place of exquisite sensations with an air of tranquillity and repose appropriate to the ablutions that would have been carried out before prayer. The supremacy of water here

Above Looking out from the Patio de la Acequia. The arches are richly decorated in *yeseria* (carved plaster) from the fourteenth century.

Left Green architecture in the shape of clipped cypress hedges in the Jardines Nuevos. A mimosa blooms in the foreground.

is a reminder that life would not exist without it, and in its purity it serves as a symbol of paradise. At the same time, the garden draws on a long Greco-Roman hydraulic tradition; the Islamic kingdom of Al-Andalus followed by a few centuries after the Roman province of Bética, and inherited devices perfectly adapted to the land and its climate.

After the Christian conquest of Granada, the Generalife passed to a Muslim convert and later to an Italian family, the Grimaldi Pallavicini, before entering state ownership in 1921 after a long lawsuit. The Italian owner created the Upper Garden in the nineteenth century, a series of terraces where hedges, rose bushes and magnolias are a perfect expression of romantic taste. Avenues of oleander and cypress also date from this period.

After the state took over the Generalife, the extensive network of fields and pastures around the old *almunia* (the Arabic word for this sort of agricultural estate) began to be converted into gardens. The New Gardens, which lie between the Alhambra and the Generalife, were developed in the 1950s by the architect and conservationist Francisco Prieto Moreno. These highly architectural spaces, structured around clipped cypresses, are inspired by Italian models, but find room for local elements including paved paths and brightly coloured pots.

The result of a continuous process of transformation, these are truly archetypal Spanish gardens, springing from a melting pot of influences and expressing their own history, as well as the history of their times.

Left The Patio del Ciprés de la Sultana (Patio of the Sultana's Cypress), whose U-shaped pool, dating from the sixteenth century, occupies the former site of the palace baths.

Right The Escalera de Agua, an original Nasrid element where water from the Acequia Real flows into channels formed by upturned tiles on top of low walls. The staircase is divided into three flights by low fountains.

CARMEN DE LA FUNDACIÓN RODRÍGUEZ-ACOSTA

Granada

The product of an artist's soul, this exquisite pairing of architecture and garden is the result of an extraordinary balance of art and nature, classical and modern, East and West. The building's white walls combine with green cypresses to frame dramatic views of the surrounding Sierra Nevada and the plain of Granada.

The place is also known as El Carmen Blanco (The White Villa), a *carmen* being a small villa with a garden, half rural and half urban, and typical of Granada. The villa is a modern, personal interpretation of this native style, built by the wealthy painter José María Rodríguez-Acosta as a studio between 1914 and 1924. Since the painter's death it has housed the eponymous foundation dedicated to the promotion and protection of the arts and sciences.

The garden's hilltop position, terraced layout and placement of the main entry at the highest side follow traditional forms dating from the Moorish period. The garden's design also flows along traditional lines, with different levels linked by flights of steps to create enclosed spaces reached by shady paths.

Above A twentieth-century bust in a corner of the garden redolent of the classical world.

Right The Jardín del Estanque de Venus (Garden of the Pool of Venus), presided over by a copy of a Roman sculpture of the goddess of love.

Left The main patio at the entrance to the villa.

Below The base of a column serves as a plinth for this Roman statue of Apollo.

What distinguishes this from the traditional *carmen*, apart from the audacious use of the great white blocks in the house's design, which echoes Viennese Secession style, is the choice of plants. These are almost entirely limited to box (*Buxus sempervirens*), myrtle (*Myrtus communis*) and cypress (*Cupressus sempervirens*), clipped in geometric shapes to form a kind of living architecture, which imparts a calm classical air to the whole. Cypress is the quintessential Mediterranean plant, used in Greek and Roman traditions and, with its vertical form, which seems to reach for the heavens, a symbol of eternity. The cypresses'

massive dark green forms perfectly complement the pure white statues and architectural elements, which include columns, porticoes and pergolas.

Some of these pieces are original, while others are copies of classical or Renaissance originals, following the style of an Italian garden. One of the most notable spaces is El Jardín di Apolo (Garden of Apollo), where an original statue of a faun is surrounded by an exedra, bringing to mind Hadrian's Villa in Rome. Another outstandingly beautiful space is the pool, with a statue of Venus copied from a classical original. Sticking faithfully to the *carmen*'s traditional

design, water plays a major part throughout the garden, in pools, basins and fountains. A further highlight is the romantic Nun's Garden, where a Renaissance-style Castilian sepulchre is surrounded by cypresses.

This is a very complex layout, with terraces and linked gardens which you often come upon by surprise. Each space offers a new view of the surroundings, creating an exceptional compound of man and nature, past and present. The white towers and dark cypresses seem to be so much a part of the landscape that it is as though they have sprung spontaneously from it.

Above Hedges structure the garden on the lower terrace.

Above left A twentieth-century statue of Diana the huntress by Pablo Liozaga animates this architectural space.

Above right El Templo de Psiquis (Psyche's Temple), with the city of Granada beyond.

REAL ALCÁZAR

Seville

This sublime collection of gardens, patios and architecture is a journey through the soul of Seville; beguiling and diverse, it represents a fusion of the cultures that shaped the city's art and history. Expansively developed in harmony with the surrounding architecture, the gardens at the Real Alcázar (Royal Palace) are a succession of spaces in various styles contained within the walled citadel. They have been altered and replanted a number of times, according to each era's tastes. Despite this accretion of space and time, the place still retains something of the captivating atmosphere of the ancient Hispano-Islamic gardens, with an abundance of delightfully intimate corners conceived for pleasure.

The word *alcázar* derives from the Arabic *al-qasr* for 'fortress'. The first fortified palace here dates from the tenth century, and was built by Moorish rulers on an old Roman settlement, which had then been occupied by the Visigoths. One of the most fascinating parts of the garden survives from this era. It was constructed under the

Left A view of the gardens from the upper walkway in the Galleria de Grutescos (Gallery of Grotesques) created in the seventeenth century by Vermondo Resta on the ancient Almohad period wall.

Above A fountain topped with a statue of Mercury by Diego de Pesquera presides over his pool.

Below Bitter orange trees (*Citrus aurantium*) in the Jardín del Chorro.

twelfth-century Almohad dynasty in what was to become centuries later the House of Trade for the Indies. The garden is cross shaped, the beds positioned lower than the surrounding walkways, so that the fruits and scented flowers of the orange trees remain within reach, while the lower level remains cool and shady – a sophisticated solution to the summer's heat. The Patio del Yeso (Plaster Patio) and Jardín de María de Padilla (Maria de Padilla's Garden) also date from this time.

The Islamic gardens were reused and transformed after the Christian conquest of Seville in 1248, when the Alcázar became the palace of Fernando 'the Holy'. (In fact, it is the oldest continuously occupied royal palace in Europe.) Traces of Gothic architecture from the reign of Alfonso X date from this early Christian era, but far more important are the *mudéjar* elements from the reigns of Alfonso XI and particularly Pedro I 'the Cruel' in the fourteenth century. The term *mudéjar* refers to the work of Muslims who were permitted to stay in the newly Christian territory, a unique fusion of the oriental and occidental. The garden created by Pedro I in 1366 has recently been rediscovered,

Above right The twelfth-century Almohad garden, with paths raised above the planting beds.

Below right Charles V's pavilion, built for his wedding to Isabel of Portugal in 1543.

Below far right A pool with sixteenth-century tiles, in the Jardin de las Flores.

having been hidden under marble paving for 400 years. A curious sunken garden with a central pool and planted borders edged with interlaced brickwork, it exemplifies the Christian king's fascination with the Hispano-Islamic world. This spirit of fusion still animates the Alcázar's gardens.

With the coming of the Habsburg dynasty in the sixteenth century, the Royal Palace and its gardens entered another heyday. The ancient orchards were transformed into Italianate gardens, at first in accordance with Renaissance precepts and later in a mannerist style. In 1546 the Emperor Charles V converted an old Muslim oratory into an exquisite pavilion which combined Renaissance style with a *mudéjar* heritage palpable in the clean tiles and the ground-level fountain.

In the early seventeenth century, in the reign of Philip III, the Milanese architect Vermondo Resta used the old Almohad wall to make the mannerist Galería de los Grutescos (Gallery of Grotesques), creating a covered walkway which still allows a view of the gardens. This is an ideal spot to enjoy the winter sun, up above the damp ground, but with a marvellous perspective on the whole layout. Next to the Galería an old irrigation tank was transformed into an elegant pool presided over by Mercury, the god of commerce. This was not an accidental choice, as in those days Seville – 'puerto y puerta de América' (America's port and portal) – was the burgeoning world capital of commerce, thanks to its monopoly of New World trade. The

flow of American gold funded these ambitious new works. The new gardens were grander and more palatial, very different to their intimate and enclosed Hispano-Islamic antecedents. Architectural elements were now included – grottoes, flights of stairs, porticoes – and other elements typical of the period such as myrtle hedges clipped into the forms of mythological figures with heads and hands of wood and clay, and ground-level water spouts to surprise passers-by.

At the beginning of the twentieth century, during the reign of Alfonso XIII, the orchards around the Alcázar were transformed again into new gardens, including a cypress and myrtle maze which replaced an earlier one, and the Jardín Inglés or English Garden – with groves and lawns – which looks quite out of place here. In this period a great many trees were introduced, including the omnipresent palms which break up the horizontality of the ancient spaces. El Jardín del Marqués de la Vega Inclán (the Marquis of Vega's Garden) was made in 1914, following the vernacular style introduced by Forestier (see Parque de María Luisa, page 232).

The conservator of the Alcázar gardens, Joaquin Murube, who created the Jardín de los Poetas (the Poets' Garden) in the 1940s, summed up the essence of these 1,000-year-old spaces in verse: 'What is the smell of the Alcázar gardens? It isn't this flower, or this leaf, or that tree, or that branch. It smells of old gardens. Of years, of centuries of gardens. Time interred, beauty fixed . . .'

Above The maze, dating from 1913, replaced an earlier one in the same place.

Left A twentieth-century design inspired by ancient Hispano-Islamic models.

Following pages The Jardín de las Damas (Garden of the Ladies) with hedges of euonymus and myrtle (*Myrtus communis*) and mock orange (*Philadelphus*) in flower.

LA CASA DE PILATOS

Seville

Even among Seville's many unforgettable patios and gardens, these ones belonging to La Casa de Pilatos (Pilate's House) are outstanding. More than five hundred years old, house and gardens are an exceptional synthesis of Spain's long history of cultures and styles, bringing together Islamic, Christian and Renaissance influences.

The house is undoubtedly a masterpiece of Spanish sixteenth-century architecture. A Renaissance style incorporates Gothic and *mudéjar* elements. (Islamic traditions of working in wood, stucco and tiles went on to inform Christian tastes.)

The house was begun in 1483 on what had been agricultural land with its own supply of water from the Roman aqueduct known as Caños de Carmona (Pipes of Carmona), a rare privilege given that this water was the near-exclusive property of the Crown.

However, the current appearance of La Casa de Pilatos owes most to the 1st Marquis of Tarifa, who passed through Italy on a pilgrimage to Jerusalem of 1518–20 and was greatly impressed by what he saw of the Renaissance, then at its height. This infatuation led him to undertake major alterations to the house, whose curious name also dates from the same visit to the Holy Land, as on his return to

This pool was originally the house's private water supply, drawn from the Carmona acqueduct. The fountain with a sculpture of young Bacchus is by Mariano Benlliure, and dates from the early twentieth century.

227

Seville the marquis ascertained that
the distance between the ruins of
Pontius Pilate's house and Golgotha
(the place of Christ's crucifixion)
matched the distance between his
house and the shrine of Cruz del
Campo, or Country Cross, outside
the city walls.

His heir, the Duke of Alcalá de
los Gazules, Viceroy of Naples, also
found his great passion for archeology
in Italy, sponsoring excavations and
acquiring entire collections. Thinking
of retiring to Spain, from 1568 the
duke began to send pieces to Seville
as well as to his Ribera Palace in
Bornos, along with his architect
Benvenuto Tortello and the sculptor
and restorer Guiliano Meniquini.

At La Casa de Pilatos Tortello
created what the historian Vicente

Above A fountain carved in Genoa
in 1529 presides over the main patio.
Bougainvillea spills over the arch in
the foreground.

Left This staircase lined with pots of
dwarf roses leads up from the Jardín
Grande.

Below A classical sculpture of a boy with an eagle in the Jardín Chico (Little Garden).

Following pages Mock orange (*Philadelphus*) blooms in the Jardín Chico with the open gallery known as the Corridor del Zaquizamí beyond.

Lleo called 'an antiquarian garden'. Very fashionable in the sixteenth and seventeenth centuries, such a garden was conceived as an open-air gallery, where regular lines of myrtle combine with flower beds and Roman artifacts.

The Italian architect's work can still be seen in what is today known as the Jardín Grande (Big Garden), a rectangular space that was previously used for growing fruit and vegetables. Tortello created three loggias with recesses and vaulted niches to display classical sculptures, around an open space planted with low clipped hedges. While the central fountain dates from this period, an iron pavilion covered by jasmine dates from a renovation of 1850, when the garden acquired the romantic character still evident today. At this time the exotic species typical of the age were planted: palm, magnolia, bougainvillea and canna.

A smaller garden, El Jardín Chico, originally occupied the space in front of the *zaquizamí*, a small pavilion housing classical pieces with three open sides for looking out to the garden, in the Hispano-Islamic tradition. The demolition of a patio in the early twentieth century added space from the upper level to this garden, whose pool is the original reservoir for water drawn from the Roman aqueduct. Today it glows with cheerful pots, those essential elements of the Sevillian garden.

Recent restoration has returned La Casa de Pilatos to its former splendour, and it now combines its function as the family residence of the ducal house of Medinaceli with being one of the essential sights for any visitor to Seville in search of beauty and history.

This is a place of pleasure. Exterior fuses with interior to form a whole that is imbued with sensuality: the murmur of water, the intense colours of bougainvillea, the delicate perfume of orange blossom . . . It is a garden of gardens that enfolds the visitor in a symphony of different forms of beauty.

EL PARQUE DE MARÍA LUISA
Seville

'A garden today is more than a luxury: it responds to contemporary needs, it has a positive role in society. Gardens are needed everywhere, from the factory to the castle, from the proudest dwelling to the humblest,' declared the French town planner and landscape designer Jean Claude Nicolas Forestier in 1920. In El Parque de María Luisa, Forestier (1861–1930) created the first public park in Seville, now one of the city's iconic features.

In 1911, the internationally renowned designer was given the job of transforming the old gardens at the Palace of San Telmo into a public park, which was also to provide the setting for the Hispano-American exposition of 1914, later postponed to 1929 and retitled the Ibero-American Exposition.

The baroque palace, dating from 1682, had been home to the Dukes of Montpensier in the second half of the nineteenth century. The Princess María Luisa, sister of the Spanish queen, Isabel II, moved with her husband, the son of the French King Louis-Philippe, to the Andalusian capital in the wake of the French revolution of 1848. Their romantic garden, from a design by Lecolant, was given to the people of Seville by María Luisa in 1893. This nineteenth-century garden was Forestier's point of departure.

He superimposed a new geometrical layout with monumental

Above The Pabellón Mudéjar (Mudéjar Pavilion) was built in 1914 by the historicist architect Aníbal González and now holds the Museo de Artes y Costumbres Populares (Museum of Popular Arts and Customs).

Right The Fuente de los Ranas (Fountain of Frogs) is inspired by Hispano-Islamic gardens.

axes in the French style over the earlier scenic design, preserving the winding paths and odd-shaped flower beds full of exotic species (araucarias, washingtonias, rubber plants) as well as picturesque elements such as the duck pond with its little island. He also managed to fit ancient orange groves into the main open spaces.

But more than this, Forestier was influenced by traditional Hispano-Islamic gardens such as those at the Alhambra or the Generalife. His great achievement here was to transfer the spirit of those intimate and sensual places to the much larger scale of a public park, using a grid of hedges to create a series of spaces. Parque María Luisa is a combination of the modern and the traditional, the result of a fusion between a classic European park, an Hispano-Islamic patio and a romantic garden.

Forestier's rediscovery of the Hispano-Islamic tradition was hugely influential on Spanish garden design, which now turned to its own roots for inspiration. He applied the fashion for regionalism – the search for inspiration in vernacular styles of the past – to garden design. This mode already dominated Sevillian architecture, as can be seen in the park itself, where the buildings put up for the exposition in the Plaza de América demonstrate an assortment of Gothic, *mudéjar* and Plateresque styles.

Forestier always adapted his work to its surroundings, not only from a

The Plaza de América with the Pabellón Mudéjar, flowering Judas trees (*Cercis siliquastrum*), date palms (*Phoenix dactylifera*), low fountains and euonymus hedges.

historical point of view, but also to take account of the climate by using indigenous plants. He loved fruit trees, particularly oranges, but he also planted crape myrtles, oleanders and roses, which were his particular passion (he was the creator of the Rose Garden at the Jardins de Bagatelle in Paris), and scented plants, including jasmine, mimosa and honeysuckle.

Plants are not the park's only important features: there are traditional ceramics, pergolas, terraces and steps, and of course water in pools and fountains throughout the garden. 'In dry lands, where the summers are parched, water is the most essential and valuable element. Its delightful presence is amplified by little jets, and it is held in marble and dazzling ceramics, so that its clean freshness is all the more evident.'

The park opened in 1914 (with further extensions in 1915 and 1924) and was soon a firm favourite with Sevillanos, as was Forestier, who became one of Spain's most sought-after designers for both public and private gardens.

The park is like another world, a bright, sensual cathedral of greenery, full of scent, colour and sound: a real tonic for the soul. As Forestier put it, 'A garden is the most restorative thing of all, preventative medicine for any kind of physical or mental ailment.'

Top Forestier considered pergolas an essential feature in gardens in warm climates. *Spiraea cantoniensis* blooms in the foreground.

Above French and Hispano-Islamic elements come together in the Glorieta de Juana Reina (Queen Juana's Bower).

Right A design based on hedges of euonymus, bitter orange (*Citrus aurantium*) and date palms (*Phoenix dactylifera*).

LA CASA DEL REY MORO
Ronda

Clinging to a narrow spit of land between the deep gorge of the river Guadalevín and the old town of Ronda, this fusion of garden and viewpoint is like a great balcony overlooking the surrounding landscape.

The French designer Jean Claude Nicolas Forestier (see also El Parque de María Luisa, page 232) made this garden for the Duchess of Parcent in 1912. This was the first of Forestier's Spanish gardens; he went on to design several others during the first decades of the twentieth century.

Enchanted by the ancient town, the duchess had acquired the eighteenth-century mansion as a place where she could spend spring and autumn away from Madrid. Known as La Casa del Rey Moro (The House of the Moorish King), it was believed locally to have been built much earlier, in the Moorish period. What does survive from that

Above Waterlilies (*Nymphaea*) and umbrella papyrus (*Cyperus alternifolius*) grow in the pool on the garden's lowest level.

Right The third terrace with splendid views out over the mountainous countryside. In the foreground are pots of pelargoniums.

Above The water channel is the garden's central axis, uniting its several levels.

Right Water descends from a tank on the highest level.

Left Water flows though a spout in the form of a lion's head into the pool on the lower terrace.

Below The low ceramic fountain on the upper terrace was inspired by Hispano-Islamic models.

time is the enigmatic Mine, a narrow staircase carved from the sheer rock face, which leads down from the house to the river at the foot of the gorge, an impregnable defence in its day.

The garden acknowledges its Moorish heritage in the use of bricks, tiles and water channels. Always keen on local traditions, Forestier used Hispano-Islamic elements and ideas, reinterpreting them and fusing them with his own French sensibility. This 'neo-Arabic' or 'neo-Sevillian' style was new to Spanish gardens, though it had already left an impression on the architecture of the period.

Although the past was a constant source of inspiration for Forestier, he did not lapse into pastiche. He wrote in *Gardens: Notebooks with Drawings and Plans* in 1920: 'Precisely because

of the need to be original and true to himself, the master gardener is aware of the past – he is inspired by it, but does not copy it. He lives in the present and develops his principles in harmony with the spirit of modernity.'

This duality is immediately apparent on entering the garden. The classical layout has a typically French emphasis on perspective, while the emblematic elements of an Andalusian garden are all in place: a low fountain, brick paving, pots.

Forestier had trained as an engineer, and creating a garden on this narrow strip of land took all his ingenuity. The result is highly architectural, with intimate spaces opening up to wide views. The garden is laid out over three levels linked by double flights of steps, and small

parterres are outlined by myrtle hedges. Another of Forestier's characteristic touches is the pergola which creates an agreeable shady corner – considered by him a particularly 'Latin' element.

When it came to planting, Forestier tended towards traditional species like myrtle, cypress, lagerstroemia, laurel, pomegranate and rose, which he combined with other species almost unknown in Spanish gardens of the time such as wisteria and pittosporum.

This is an orderly space, but full of welcoming nooks. As you stroll through it, Forestier's words come to mind: 'Gardens are subtle works of art, made up of poetry and architecture, art and nature. They bring opposites together: delicacy and audacity, simplicity and ingenuity, regularity and fantasy, rigour and abandon.'

LA CONCEPCIÓN
Málaga

Entering La Concepción you forget the parched and rugged landscape of Málaga and find yourself in a dense and exotic forest, mysterious and magical. Conrad's description in *Heart of Darkness* of 'travelling back to the earliest beginnings of the world, when vegetation rioted on the earth and big trees were kings' comes to mind. But you could not be further from the wild and menacing African jungle Conrad described: La Concepción, like any garden, is a domesticated and unthreatening version of nature, shaped by the hand of its creators and their times.

Málaga in the mid-nineteenth century was a prosperous city with a thriving port, the second most important industrial region in Spain.

Left and above Covered in Chinese wisteria (*Wisteria sinensis*), the massive iron pergola next to the house is sensational in April when the wisteria fills the atmosphere with an explosion of colour and delicate perfume.

243

Among the many cosmopolitan residents was the wealthy entrepreneur Jorge Loring Oyarzábal, of North American parentage, and his wife, Amalia Heredia Livermore. The couple bought the land in 1857 for a country estate and set about creating this romantic tropical garden, which in its day hosted leading social events, political meetings and cultural salons: it was to be a private paradise, far from the city and its factories.

The abundant, exuberant vegetation takes centre stage here. Through their international business contacts the founders obtained species from five continents: strelitzias, rubber trees, araucarias, cyclades, dragon trees and a splendid collection of fifty different species of palm. Plants that elsewhere in Europe would only be found in glasshouses flourish cheerfully here in the area's famously benign microclimate.

The couple found a Frenchman, Jacint Chamousset, to turn their dreams into reality. He laid out through the dense vegetation a network of mazy paths, which,

Left The cascade is ringed by Swiss cheese plants (*Monstera deliciosa*).

Above right The garden is characterized by its exuberant growth of exotic species, creating shady and jungle-like corners.

Below right The Fuente de La Ninfa (Fountain of the Nymph) pours water into a pond full of waterlilies.

typically for a garden of the period, led to intriguing set pieces: a bamboo forest, a cascade and a Doric temple. Built in 1860 by a Prussian architect, Strack, the temple held the extensive archaeological collection of the now ennobled Marquis of Casa-Loring. Another notable stop on any tour is the monumental wrought-iron arbour next to the house, spectacular in spring when the wisteria flowers.

Following the death of its founders in the early twentieth century, La Concepción was acquired by a Basque couple, Amalia Echevarrieta and Rafael Echevarría, who extended the garden and created a viewpoint and the Arroyo de la Ninfa, or Nymph's Stream. Since 1990 the estate has been owned by the City of Málaga. With its massive old trees and miraculously fresh shade, this is a place quite unlike any other on the Costa del Sol.

Bougainvillea surrounds the garden's entrance.

INFORMATION FOR VISITORS

ATLANTIC

PAZO DE MARIÑÁN
Calle Bergondo
15165 La Coruña
Tel. 981 777 001
www.visitapazo.com

MONASTERIO DE SAN LORENZO DE
TRASOUTO
Calle de San Lorenzo
15705 Santiago de Compostela
Tel. 981 552 725
www.pazodesanlorenzo.com

PAZO DE CASTRELOS
Parque de Castrelos
36213 Vigo
Tel. 986 29 59 75

LA QUINTA
Fundación Selgas-Fagalde
La Quinta
El Pito
33154 Cudillero
Tel. 985 59 01 20
www.selgas-fagalde.com

SEÑORÍO DE BÉRTIZ
Parque Natural Señorío de Bértiz
Oieregi Bertizarana
31720 Navarra
Tel. 948 592 421
www.parquedebertiz.es

JARDÍN DE ACLIMATACIÓN DE LA
OROTAVA
Calle Retama, no. 2
38400 Puerto de La Cruz, Tenerife
Tel. 922 389 464

JARDÍN DE LA MARQUESA DE
ARUCAS
Ctra GC 330 Arucas-Bañaderos, Km 2
35400 Gran Canaria
Tel. 928 604 486
www.jardindelamarquesa.com

JARDÍN DE CACTUS
Carretera Guatiza Mala LZ 1
35544 Lanzarote
Tel. 928 845 398
www.fcmanrique.org

MEDITERRANEAN

JARDINES ARTIGAS
Alfores – Cami de la Pobla
a Clot del Moro
08696 La Pobla de Lillet
Tel. 938 236146
www.gaudiallgaudi.com

PARK GÜELL
Calle Olot, no. 5
08024 Barcelona
Tel. 93 413 24 00
www.gaudiallgaudi.com

LABERINTO DE HORTA
Calle Germans Desvalls
08035 Barcelona
Tel. 93 265 56 01
www.parcsijardins.cat

PARQUE SAMÁ
Ctra. T-314 Vinyols i els Arcs
43850 Cambrils
Tel. 977 826 5 14
www.parc-sama.es

JARDÍN DE MONTFORTE
Plaza de la Legión Española
46010 Valencia
Tel. 96 352 54 78 ext 1184

HUERTO DEL CURA
Porta de la Morera, no. 49
03203 Elche
Tel. 965 45 19 36
www.huertodelcura.com

RAIXA
Carretera Palma-Sóller, Km 12
07110 Mallorca
Tel. 971 17 38 44
www.raixa.cat

ALFABIA
Carretera Palma-Sóller, Km 17
07110 Mallorca
Tel. 971 613 123
www.jardinesdealfabia.com

PEDRERES DE S'HOSTAL
Camino Viejo, Km 1
07760 Ciudadela Menorca
Tel. 971 48 15 78
www.lithica.es

THE CENTRE

PALACIO REAL DE LA GRANJA DE
SAN ILDELFONSO
Plaza de España
40100 Real Sitio de San Ildelfonso
Tel. 921-47 00 19
www.patrimonionacional.es

EL ROMERAL DE SAN MARCOS
Calle Marqués de Villena, no. 6
40003 Segovia
Tel. 921 44 13 79

EL BOSQUE
Calle Obispo Zarranz y Pueyo, no. 58
37700 Béjar
Tel. 923 404 528

REAL MONASTERIO DE SAN
LORENZO
DE EL ESCORIAL
Calle de Juan de Borbón y
Battemberg
28200 San Lorenzo de El Escorial
Tel. 91 890 59 03
www.patrimonionacional.es

CASITA DEL PRÍNCIPE
Ctra Villalba-Escorial, Km 56
28200 San Lorenzo de El Escorial
Tel. 91 890 59 03
www.patrimonionacional.es

CASITA DEL INFANTE
Ctra de Ávila
28200 San Lorenzo de El Escorial
Tel. 91 890 59 03
www.patrimonionacional.es

LA QUINTA DEL DUQUE DEL ARCO
Ctra del Pardo
28048 El Pardo
Tel. 91 376 21 56
www.patrimonionacional.es

JARDINES DEL BUEN RETIRO
Plaza Independencia, no. 1
28014 Madrid
Tel. 91 273 39 88
www.parquedelretiro.com

JARDÍN DE JOAQUÍN SOROLLA
Avenida General Martínez Campos,
no. 37
28010 Madrid
Tel. 91 310 15 84
www.museosorolla.mcu.es

REAL JARDÍN BOTÁNICO
Plaza de Murillo, no. 2
28014 Madrid
Tel. 91 420 30 17
www.rjb.csic.es

EL CAPRICHO
Paseo de la Alameda de Osuna
28042 Madrid
Tel. 915880104

REAL SITIO DE ARANJUEZ
Plaza de Parejas
28300 Aranjuez
Tel. 91 8910740
www.patrimonionacional.es

JARDIN DE LA REAL FÁBRICA DE
PAÑOS
Paseo de la fábrica
19400 Brihuega
Tel. 949 28 04 42

MONASTERIO DE PIEDRA
50210 Nuévalos
Tel. 976 84 90 11
www.monasteriodepiedra.com

ANDALUSIA

EL PATIO DE LOS NARANJOS
Calle Cardenal Herrero, no. 1
14003 Córdoba
Tel. 957 47 05 12
www.mezquitadecordoba.org

PALACIO DE VIANA
Plaza Don Gómez, no. 2
14001 Córdoba
Tel. 957 49 67 41
www.fundacioncajasur.com

LA ALHAMBRA
Calle Real de la Alhambra
18009 Granada
Tel. 902 441 221
www.alhambra-patronato.es

EL GENERALIFE
Calle Real de la Alhambra
18009 Granada
Tel. 902 441 221
www.alhambra.org

CARMEN DE LA FUNDACIÓN
RODRÍGUEZ-ACOSTA
Calle Niños del Rollo, no. 8
Granada 18009
Tel. 958 227 497
www.fundacionrodriguezacosta.com

REAL ALCÁZAR
Patio de Banderas
41004 Sevilla
Tel. 954 502 323
www.patronato-alcazarsevilla.es

LA CASA DE PILATOS
Plaza de Pilatos no. 1
41003 Sevilla
Tel. 954 225 298
www.fundacionmedinaceli.org

EL PARQUE DE MARÍA LUISA
41000 Sevilla
Tel. 954 23 73 38
www.parquedemarialuisa.es

LA CASA DEL REY MORO
Cuesta de Santo Domingo, no. 9
29600 Ronda
Tel. 952 187 200
www.palacioreymoro.com

LA CONCEPCIÓN
Camino del Jardín Botánico, no. 3
29014 Málaga
Tel. 952 250 745
www.laconcepcion.malaga.eu

BIBLIOGRAPHY

These books have been my travelling companions during my journey through the great gardens of Spain.

Añón, Carmen and José Luis Sancho (ed.), *Jardín y Naturaleza en el reinado de Felipe II*, Ediciones Doce Calles, Aranjuez, 1998

Añón, Carmen, and Mónica and Ana Luengo, *Jardines Artísticos de España*, Espasa Calpe, Madrid, 1995

Baridon, Michel, *Los Jardines Paisajistas, Jardineros, Poetas*, Abada Editores, Madrid, 2005

Bassegoda, Joan, Ramón Espel and Roger Orriols, *Gaudí a la Vall de Lillet*, Amalgama Edicions, Berga, 2002

Bassegoda Nonell, Juan, *Aproximación a Gaudí*, Ediciones Doce Calles, Aranjuez, 1992

Brown, Jane, *The Pursuit of Paradise*, Harper Collins, London, 2000

Byne, A. and M. Stapley, *Casas y Jardines de Mallorca*, Editor José J. de Olañeta, Palma de Mallorca, 1999

Carandell, Josep, *Park Güell. Utopía de Gaudí*, Triangle Postals SL, Sant Lluis, 1998

Casa Valdés, Marquesa de, *Jardines de España*, Editorial Aguilar, Madrid, 1973

Correcher, Consuelo M., *The Gardens of Spain*, Harry N. Abrams Inc., New York, 1993

Durán Cermeño, Consuelo, *Jardines del Buen Retiro*, Ediciones Doce Calles, Aranjuez, 2002

Fernández Álvarez, Manuel, *Felipe II*, Espasa Calpe, Madrid, 2005

Forestier, J.C.N., *Jardines, cuadernos de dibujos y planos*, Editorial Stylos, Madrid, 1985

García Gómez, Francisco, *La Concepción, Testigo del Tiempo*, Arguval, Málaga, 2004

Gaudí, Antoni, *Manuscritos, Artículos, Conversaciones, Dibujos*, Colección de Arquitectura 6, Colegio Oficial de Aparejadores y Arquitectos Técnicos de Murcia, 2002

Gómez Aguilera, Fernando, *Cesar Manrique en sus palabras*, Fundación César Manrique, Taro de Tahiche, 1995

Guía de Aranjuez, Ediciones Doce Calles, Aranjuez, 1999

Joyce, David (ed.), *Garden Styles*, Pyramid Books, London, 1989

Leclerc, Béndedicte (ed.) *Jean Claude Nicolas Forestier 1861–1930: Du jardin au paysage urbain*, Picard éditeur, Paris, 1994

Mosser, Monique and Georges Teyssot (ed.), *The History of Garden Design*, Thames and Hudson, London, 2000

Murria, Donald, Jaume Llabrés and Aiana Pascual, *Jardines de Mallorca*, Editor José J. de Olañeta, Palma de Mallorca, 2003

Ramírez de Lucas, Juan, *Jardín de Cactus*, Ed Fundación César Manrique, Taro de Tahiche, 2000

Revilla, Uceda and Angel Miguel, *José María Rodríguez-Acosta 1878–1941*, Turner Libros, Madrid, 1994

Rodríguez, Dacal and Jesús Carlos y Izco, *El Pazo de Mariñán*, Diputación Provincial de A Coruña, La Coruña, 1998

El Romeral de San Marcos. Un jardín de Leandro Silva, Caja de Ahorros de Segovia, Segovia, 2002

Sancho, José Luis, *Jardines Reales de España*, Ediciones Aldeasa, 2006

Segura Munguía, Santiago, *Los Jardines de la Antigüedad*, Universidad de Deusto, Bilbao, 2005

Valdeón Menéndez, José, *Jardines Clásicos de Asturias*, Cajastur, Oviedo, 1999

Von Buttlar, Adrian, *Jardines del Clasicismo y el Romanticismo*, Ed Nerea, Madrid, 1993

Winthuysen, Xavier de, *Jardines Clásicos de España*, edición en facsímil de la edición original de 1930, Ediciones Doce Calles, Aranjuez 1990

INDEX

Illustrations generally appear on the same pages as the text. Illustrations and captions separated from the text are given page references in **bold**.

ACKNOWLEDGEMENTS

First of all, thank you to the owners of the private gardens in this book: to the Duques de Soma, the family of Benítez de Lugo, the Marqués de Marianao, the Zaforteza family and Julia Casardevilla for their generous collaboration, also to María del Mar Junco at the Fundación Selgas-Fagalde, to Laetitia Sauleau at La Asociación Lítica and to Cristina Rodríguez Acosta at the Fundación Rodríguez-Acosta. To María Eugenia Pernas, Mr and Mrs Bahamonde, Miguel Cabrera, Juan de Orbaneja, José Antonio Cañizo, César Requesens, and Mercedes del Castillo for their advice. A very special thank you to María Jesús Cagiga and Luisa Roquero for their erudite suggestions. My sincerest gratitude to Jo Christian for her patience and support, to Andrew Dunn for his careful translation and to Maria Charalambous for her delicate and elegant design. And to Pelayo, Gaspar and León Mencos Bojstad, 'collateral victims' of their parents' passion for gardens.

This book is for Pelayo, Gaspar and León, sweet and beloved fruits of the garden of our life.